RON WOOD
The Works

RON WOOD
The Works

BY RON WOOD
WITH BILL GERMAN

1817

HARPER & ROW, PUBLISHERS, NEW YORK
Cambridge, Philadelphia, San Francisco, Washington
London, Mexico City, São Paulo, Singapore, Sydney

FIRST EDITION

Designer: Barbara Richer

Copyeditor: Daril Bentley

Library of Congress Cataloging-in-Publication Data

Wood, Ron, 1947–
Ron Wood: the works.

1. Wood, Ron, 1947–   2. Rock musicians—England—Biography.   I. German, Bill.   II. Title.
ML419.W66A3   1987   784.5'4'00924 [B]   86-45164
ISBN 0-06-096098-1 (pbk.)
                                        87 88 89 90 91 RRD 10 9 8 7 6 5 4 3 2 1
ISBN 0-06-055100-3 (lim. ed.)

1

*I*n the back of my head I always knew I'd be a musician first and an artist later. My older brothers eventually chose art over music for their careers, but they made good money as musicians playing clubs and touring around. (Their band even played Poland.)

The moment I made any kind of money from my music, I knew the windfalls were not far behind. Let's face it, it took Elvis a few months to sell a million records, while Van Gogh sold just one painting during his whole life. My choice was easy. Hardly anyone makes money from their art until they're dead. From my point of view, it's definitely an advantage to enjoy your wealth while you're still alive.

My earliest performing experience came with my school's four-piece madrigal choir. First I was treble, then tenor, then alto. Finally, after reaching puberty, I was baritone and bass. But my big break in the music biz came when I was only nine years old. My brothers' band had this gig at the local movie theater, playing in between two Tommy Steele flicks, and they let me come onstage to play washboard. That was the first time I experienced butterflies in the stomach. I almost peed in my pants.

I fooled around with all sorts of instruments that my brothers stored in the back room of the house. Washboards, trumpets, banjos, kazoos. But I knew guitar was my thing. Whenever I would see someone play guitar, I'd get the itch to pick one up myself. Believe me, I saw some great guitarists play with my brothers. They had these two guys, Jim Willis and Lawrence Sheaf, who really helped me learn how to play. Jim taught me

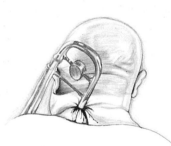

DEATH BY TROMBONE

the fundamentals, writing out all the chords and fingering techniques, and Lawrence showed me how to play all this great Big Bill Broonzy stuff. I was introduced to the music of Louis Armstrong, Bix Beiderbeck, and Jellyroll Morton by my brother Ted. He's still a jazz purist to this day. Keeps all his old records in perfect condition. My brother Art, however, crossed over to R&B and rockabilly, starting his own band, the Artwoods. Art took me to some great shows at a club called Railway Arms, and he started teaching me the basic chords to songs like "Midnight Special," "I'm Walkin'," and "Great Balls of Fire." My brothers encouraged me a great deal. In fact, they bought me my first guitar. Wait, that's not true. My first guitar was actually *given* to me by this guy, Chalkie White. But when he went into the Army, he took his guitar with him. I was about ten years old. My brothers felt bad about it, so they chipped in to replace it, and at last I had my very own guitar.

My first band was called The Birds. It consisted of Ali McKenzie as lead vocal, Tony Munroe and me on guitar, Kim Gardner on bass, and Pete McDaniels on drums. We were no relation to the "Turn, Turn, Turn" Byrds from America. In fact, the funniest thing happened when those Byrds, who *were* much bigger than us, came over to London in 1965. The minute they stepped off the plane, our manager handed them a summons, demanding that they change their name, and claiming that we had lost work because of the confusion. It was really just a publicity stunt and it made the papers. I think it may have even overshadowed some of our real accomplishments.

Early on, The Birds opened up our own club in West Drayton, called The Nest. It was actually the neighborhood community center, which provided free facilities for social events. We convinced them to let us play there every Friday, charge a nominal admission fee, and call the place The Birds Nest for one night a week. They said if we could fill the place, we could stay on. We gradually built up a pretty big local following. People like the late Phil Lynott and Lemmy from Motorhead used to come watch us all the time.

I remember how we would wheel the equipment in on wheelbarrows. I rented an electric guitar for 25 quid to use onstage. The songs we played were all covers of American artists: Chuck Berry, Bo Diddley, Howlin' Wolf, tons of Motown. A lot of so-called "black music." White working-class kids in England were

going through a lot of the same stuff as black kids in the States, so I guess that's why we had similar tastes in music.

Funny enough, we also copied Stones songs. And Beatles, of course. Both those groups were themselves incorporating that black music into their original material. Eventually, I started writing original songs for the group, and we got real popular. (Um, not that my songs were totally responsible, but . . .) We began playing clubs in other towns, where we'd bump into other great bands on the circuit like The Yardbirds, The Pretty Things, and The Stones. Robert Stigwood started managing us, and some breaks came our way. We got a cameo role as ourselves in a forgettable film called *The Deadly Bees*. We were shown playing a song in a TV studio. Us in the background, while some murder was being plotted in the foreground. We also did the British TV show "Thank Your Lucky Stars," just

FATS DOMINO

After I'd been fed a steady dose of jazz from my brother Ted, it was Art who introduced rock 'n' roll to me. I'll never forget walking into Art's room and seeing a **78** record of Fats' "I'm Walkin'" on that big dansette phonograph. That was really the first rock song I was exposed to. All right, maybe that and "Great Balls of Fire." They were the first songs that my brothers taught me on guitar. After that, rock 'n' roll was in my blood, brother!

I did this monotype using a tiny picture as a reference. The only good picture of Fats I could find was part of some ad for a big compilation record. "Fifty artists in all!" The fuckin' picture was the size of a postage stamp! I squinted to get the detail, using one of those big magnifying glasses that kids use to look at bugs. Paul Shaffer and I playing the "Fats and Friends" cinemax special for HBO along with Jerry Lee Lewis and Ray Charles was a special honor for us. Fats signed an old photo for me, showing him and the Beatles in a dressing room.

like The Stones had done a couple years earlier. We were lowered onto the stage by wires (with our drummer landing *bang* on top of his drums!), and flew off the same way we came on. The odd thing about The Birds, though, is that despite some big singles, we never released an album.

When The Birds broke up, I played very briefly in a studio band called Santa Barbara Machine Head. It consisted of a guy named Twink on drums, Deep Purple's John Lord (who was previously in my brother's band, The Artwoods) on organ, and Kim Gardner, who was moonlighting from The Creation. Kim, the bass player, left to join The Creation. But I remained friendly with him all along. In fact, in 1968 *I* had a short stint with The Creation. We toured Germany with Diana Ross and The Supremes. *They* opened up for *us*. I Created for about three months. I mean, I had already been in the Jeff Beck Group, but in March of '68, Jeff was advised to fire me and Mickey Waller unceremoniously. After two disastrous shows with the "new" line-up, Jeff and Rod called and asked me to come back—this time on my own financial terms. The road with Beck was a rocky one.

I first bumped into Beck when I was on the club circuit with The Birds. His group The Yardbirds were one of my biggest inspirations. They were pretty hot shit. Eric Clapton was in the band then. I went to see them every week at the Crawdaddy, the happening place in Richmond. R&B like you'd never heard before. Sweat dripping from the ceilings, people swinging from the rafters. What a cooking unit! Keith Relf was a great vocalist and harmonica player. I remember that his dad drove the band to each gig. After the show he'd lecture them outside, while they were packing up. A whole critique. "You played as good, if not better than the Manfred's tonight boys."

Well, one day, Keith Relf was ill and couldn't make it to a gig. I was standing in the audience and Clapton goes up to the mike and says, "Our singer's not feeling well. Can anyone out there play harmonica?" I really wanted to get up there, but I was too scared. Eventually, all my friends pushed me on. My big break and I was pretty good. After the show the band sent for me. They patted me on the back and said I showed promise. That was how I first got friendly with Eric. And with Eric's girlfriend Krissie, who later became my wife.

When The Yardbirds fell apart, I was asked to join The New Yardbirds, who later became Led Zeppelin. But I was still pretty friendly with Beck. I rang him up and said, "Let's get a band together." He was thinking about forming a group, so it came together. We got Rod Stewart on lead vocals fresh from Steam Packet, Long John Baldrie's band. The problem was that whenever we jammed together, I played guitar. And why not? But Jeff hated that. He wanted to be the guitarist in the band. "Would you mind playin' bass?" he asked me. I went 'round to a music store called Sound City and stole a bass, because I didn't have the money to make the payments. Five or six years later, when I was in The Faces, I went there and told them, "I'm the

HOWLIN' WOLF

Considering that I never knew what the guy fuckin' looked like, this isn't such a bad representation. Okay, I'm exaggerating. What I mean is that when I first got into him, he had no exposure in Britain. His "Smokestack Lightning" was one of the first records I ever bought, but it didn't have his picture on it. No one knew what he looked like. And even though my brother's band The Artwoods used to back him up at this club called Klook's Kleek, it wasn't until 1975 that I finally met him, in Bill Wyman's hotel room in Chicago. Some of my other favorites were also in that room: Muddy Waters, Buddy Guy, and Junior Wells. We were gettin' their autographs, and Howlin' Wolf goes, "I'm not gonna sign on the same page as Muddy."

They had this sarcastic rapport with one another. It was great.

Howlin' Wolf died about a year after that incident, cashing in his chips near the end of a show. That's a pretty romantic notion for a musician like me. I mean, none of us are gettin' out of here alive, so going out onstage ain't so bad a way—in my book.

guy who stole your Fender jazz bass and I've come here to pay you." They were delighted.

But, the Jeff Beck Group didn't turn out to be the windfall that I expected. Jeff's management treated me and Rod and the rest of the guys like second-class citizens, both musically and financially. I suppose Rod didn't mind, he was just happy being around people who breathed. His first paying job was as a grave digger, you know. Actually, Rod was pretty shrewd. He always did a lot better than me, come to think of it. It all depended on how good a businessman you were. Jeff came off best, then Rod, leaving Mickey Waller, Nicky Hopkin and me struggling as best we could.

I remember the first time we hit the U.S., in '68. We played the Fillmore East in New York. (We performed so many encores that the headliners, the Grateful Dead, could only fit in a half-hour set!) Jeff Beck, of course, stayed at the Hilton while me and Rod crammed into one room at the Gorham Hotel. We were so desperate at times that we'd go down to Horn & Hardart, the automat, to steal eggs. That's how we lived. But the Gorham was actually the place to be. *Everyone* stayed there. Cream, Sly Stone, Hendrix. We met 'em all whenever we stayed there. Great energy in that place. In fact, Rod and I passed by

MUDDY WATERS

It was great playing with him a few months before he died. Mick, Keith, and I were in Chicago during our 1981 tour, and after doing a Stones show, we went to see Muddy at Buddy Guy's club, the Checkerboard Lounge. We had a great jam session, which we videotaped. Muddy and Mick dueting on "Hootchie Cootchie Man," "Mawish Boy" and "Long Distance Call" and us guitar players being truly elated by the surprise arrival of Buddy himself on stage. Even near his death, Muddy still had all the ingredients that made him the great blues innovator that he was. Very virile, bouncy, vocally and instrumentally adept right to the end.

I tell you, it's times like these that make Keith and I look at each other and say, "What? They're allowing *us* to play with Muddy?" (Or whichever one of our idols we may happen to stumble on stage with.) I mean, Muddy was one of my biggest influences in learning to play slide guitar, and there *I* was playing slide with *him!*

He lent me his very short bottleneck for the duration of "Long Distance Call." Actually, *he* was always happy to see me. Even way back, when he thought I was in The Stones, ten years before I actually joined. I met him three times and each time, he'd hug me and say to the people with him, "Hey everybody, this is my friend from The Rollinstones" (He'd pronounce it as one word). So when I bumped into him after I actually did join the band I grabbed *him* and said, "Muddy! I'm finally in that group you *thought* I was in!" He said "You can't fool me—I know you 'bin there all the time—you're Mickey Jaguar."

there a couple years ago and they had the same staff. "Ah, Mr. Wood, Mr. Stewart, it's a pleasure to see you." It blew our minds. We didn't even know the place was still standing.

Another hotel with entertainers coming and going all the time was Loew's Midtown, on Eighth Avenue. There's a restaurant next door called Wienerwald. Walking out of there once I bumped into Muhammad Ali. I ran right up to him and shook his hand. He had no idea who I was, but since I had a small entourage with me—roadies, groupies—he must've figured I was *some*body. All I said was, "I wish my dad were here now." He loved Ali.

I'm real proud of some of the work I did in the Jeff Beck Group. I still get compliments for my bass-work on "The Truth" and "Beck-Ola" albums. But after not touching a guitar for the entire time I was with Jeff, I wanted to again. By the end of 1969, it was pretty clear the Jeff Beck Group was over. So I called up Ronnie Lane and joined The Small Faces. They already had a few hits in England and were one of my few favorite bands that seemed accessible. If I was gonna keep music as a career, I figured, why not do it with people I could relate to? As much as I loved The Stones, it just didn't seem realistic for me at that time. (Little did I know that I *could* have joined The Stones in '69, which I'll discuss later.)

I was more than happy to play with The Small Faces; I was already pretty friendly with all of them, especially Steve Marriott, who I ended up replacing. He used to play with Alexis Korner, as did my brother, Art. His departure left Ronnie Lane on bass, Ian McLagan on keyboards, and Kenney Jones on drums. We still needed a proper vocalist, so I called Rod and said, "Why don't you come see this band I'm playin' with?" We were all too scared to sing, so we only did instrumentals. Rod stood at the top of the steps leading down to the studio, listening, but not watching. Afterward, he commented, "Great band." So Kenney Jones and I said, "Why don't you join?" It was as easy as that.

Ironically, we began rehearsing at the rehearsal place belonging to The Stones. Ian Stewart, who worked with The Stones and was a good friend of Ronnie Lane's, told us we could use it. (In fact, almost up to the day Stu died, Ronnie was bickering about getting Stu's permission to use The Stones' Mobile Studio.) After a few months, we decided to shorten our name to

ERIC CLAPTON

He was my first white influence. I used to see him and Beck every week at the Crawdaddy Club. One week The Stones would play, the next would be Clapton with The Yardbirds. Here was a white guy playing blues so well.

We've stayed close throughout the years. A good friend of The Stones. He gave us a lot of support when our great friend Ian Stewart died around Christmas, '85. Simon Kirke, Townshend, Beck, and Jack Bruce gave us a lot of support too. Eric came to the funeral, and afterwards we went to his house to vent ourselves by having a low-key jam session.

Eric was the natural choice to present us with our Grammy Awards in '86. He kept joking with us about how the award was for Lifetime Achievement, sort of insinuating that it's high time The Stones retired. After the Awards Keith says to me, "Hey, I heard Clapton's moving out of his flat tomorrow. Let's go over there and tear the fucking place apart!" So we zoomed over there with Mick and the place was hollow except for Eric. There was just a bed, a sofa, an exercise bike, and about five cases of Jack Daniels. We left around seven in the morning and Eric said, "Hey, what am I gonna do with all this extra booze? I gotta get outta here tomorrow." So we ran back and started stuffing our coat pockets with bottles. Anything to help Eric.

BO DIDDLEY

The only man in history to do so many songs about himself (apart from maybe Jerry Lee Lewis). But what great songs they were! Ah, Bo's wonderful. It was great jamming with him a few months back in California for a cable-TV special. Before the show, he cooked a barbecue for all the musicians and then, *during* the show, he *really* started to cook!

I think this picture came out so well because he's such a nice guy. (How's that for artistic analysis!) After the show in California, I gave him the original painting. He was blown away. He was so humble. He couldn't believe I'd actually spent the time painting it, much less be willing to give it

to him. We were both really excited by it all, and I said, "Bo, gimme your address. We'll stay in touch." So he immediately scribbled it on the back of the picture. A real bright move on my part since he wound up taking the picture with him!

I first met Bo pretty early on in my career in the mid-sixties. In fact, he gave me my first piece of advice. "I'm with Decca Records," I told him, "and they're not promoting our group. What should I do?" He said, "Tell Decca to shit or get off the pot!" When I reminded him in California about that piece of advice, he said, "Little did I know at that time that Chess Records was already flushing *me* down the toilet!"

JIMI HENDRIX

I spent some good times with Hendrix. It's all pretty hazy, though. Purple hazy! I do remember hanging out for a week at his house in London. I left with some great old blues albums, like my first copy of "BB King Live at the Regal." He also gave me a dog! A basset hound. A parting gift, I suppose. That dog could probably tell some great stories!

I played with Jimi onstage a few times in New York. We did this outdoor gig on Staten Island, and I also played with him at Steve Paul's Scene on 46th Street. It was all during my days with the Jeff Beck Group. Jimi used to convince Jeff to give me solos. He'd say, "Hey, let the bass player play."

Considering how it was with Beck, I wondered about the two guys backing Hendrix. I asked his drummer Mitch Mitchell, "How much do you guys make?"

"Let me put it to you this way," he said. "After this gig we can each buy a Porsche."

"Yeah, but is Jimi a fair man to work for?"

"Oh, sure." Then he said a classic line: "There's three of us in the band so we split everything straight down the middle."

JIMMY PAGE

I knew him from the early days, '64, '65. Everyone did. He was the number one session man—played on everyone's records. Marianne Faithfull, The Who, Cocker, the whole lot.

What most people don't know is that that thing he does, playing the guitar with a violin bow, was a technique we both shared. During my few months on tour with The Creation in '68, I was filling in for Eddie Phillips, who I believe originated the approach. So the audiences expected it from me as well. I felt a little awkward showing off like that, but it was fun.

Actually, I never considered Page self-indulgent, as some people do. He was only doing what was successful with that band at that time, all those dramatic solos. In fact, if anything, he understates himself. He doesn't rate himself very highly as a guitar player. And that's a pretty rare quality within the core of musicians from that era.

CHUCK BERRY

"Can't get away from you, can I?" That's the first thing he said to me at that Hall of Fame dinner in '86. He was right! I think Keith and I are on some sort of collision course with Chuck. But then, I suppose any guitarist so influenced by him *would* be, in some way. I first started hearing his music by seeing all the various bands my brothers were in, and they'd always be covering his stuff. Then, in *my* first band, The Birds, we covered a lot of Berry by learning from his records. I never knew what he looked like until ten years after I was into him. You never saw photos of him. It wasn't that he was black or anything, it was just that the British media was so lame and ill-informed at the time. So the content of the picture I drew here, ironically, is the image I never knew of him at the time. Those classic shots when he first made it. Although, I must say, he's remained a good-looking, rugged guy—the nicest ex-con I know.

I'm not sure if there's a way to repay someone like Chuck Berry for all that people like Keith and I have borrowed from him. But if there is a way, we'd gladly give it to him, with interest. At the Hall of Fame ceremony, Keith said, "I lifted every lick he ever played." And Chuck apologized to Keith for the hundredth time for accidentally punching him in the eye. Accidentally, folks. A case of mistaken identity. Keith snuck up behind him in a crowded club in New York, The Ritz, grabbing his shoulder, to congratulate him on a fine show, and Chuck just turned around and, WHAM! I remember Keith saying, "If anyone's gonna punch me in the eye, it's a good thing it's Chuck Berry." Keith would've demolished anyone else. For a few seconds, he contemplated slugging Chuck right back, maybe giving him a white eye! Some people think Chuck might resent how we've borrowed so much from him, but I think he's flattered. He's just a little moody sometimes, that's all.

Anyway, the funny thing about it all is that some weeks after he punched Keith, *I* went to the same club to see Chuck play again. I was standing on the side of the stage with my amp and guitar. (Let's hear it for spontaneity! I mean, I came to play with Chuck Berry even if he didn't know it.) Chuck sees me on the side of the stage, stops his show, and says, "Wait a minute. I owe this guy an apology. Keith Richards!" And he waves me over. "Well, I'm a *messenger* from Keith," I told the crowd as an aside. After the show, I kept Chuck there late. I'm sure he *still* thought I was Keith.

When I did a show with him in Irvine, California, in '85, he picked me up and hugged me. "You do know who I am?" I asked him. He said, "Sure I do." But I still wasn't convinced that he did.

He definitely knew who I was

were on the same bill as some of those older guys, they wouldn't give you the time of day. Now, Chuck got Keith to work on the "Hail! Hail! Rock 'N' Roll" movie with him. Keith went to St. Louis, where he met Chuck's father. "Dad," Chuck says, "this is a member of The Rolling Stones, the oldest surviving rock 'n' roll group." His father looks a bit surprised, takes the pipe out of his mouth, and goes, "Well, you're lookin' good!"

Anyway, I gave Chuck the drawing at that Irvine show. When he saw it, still wrapped up in paper, he commented, "That's not a picture, that's a wall partition." But he was genuinely appreciative, I think. I mean, he left the hall with just three things in his hands: his guitar, my picture, and the gig money. The three most important things for him that night. Though not necessarily in that order.

in New York when we played the scheduled Ritz show together in '86. After all, we shared the bill. First, I came out and did a few of my own songs. Then he came out and did a set with me backing him up. It was great. My little kids were there and, having seen Michael J. Fox do "Johnny B. Goode" in the movie *Back to the Future,* they said backstage, "we loved when you and that man did the Michael J. Fox song." I got Chuck to do some numbers he'd forgotten about. He was flattered that I remembered them. He's found this new respect for guys like me and Keith. I guess he just realizes that us new rock 'n' rollers have some depth, knowledge, and ability. Wait, did I say "new"? We're fuckin' forty years old, playin' for over twenty years. But I guess that's how we've earned that repect. 'Cuz in the early days, if you

The Faces. It was simply a way to separate the old configuration from the new.

The Faces did quite well. I think we were the second highest concert draw of the seventies, after The Stones. The Faces broke up in '75, after touring twice in one year. Our last studio album was "Ooh La La," in '73. Ronnie Lane had quit shortly after that, so we had to do those last tours with another bassist, Tetsu Yamauchi.

But there were no hard feelings when Ronnie quit. He had far too many brushes with Rod for me not to understand. Before The Faces' reunion concert in '86, they hadn't seen one another for over a decade. In recent years, of course, Ronnie hasn't been feeling too well. He was stricken with multiple sclerosis around '80. It was very sad and sobering to us rowdy rock 'n' rollers. That stiff dose of reality brought many musicians out in '83 in support of ARMS (Action for Research into Multiple Sclerosis). Ronnie's in good spirits now. Very dedicated to his charity foundation, and he can actually stand with the aid of a cane. But I know how painful it must be, not being able to play as well as he used to, but meanwhile Ronnie is moving from strength to strength.

The Faces did mad things right to the very end. On the last Faces tour in '75—this is already after my first tour with The Stones—we were sitting on a beach in Honolulu. (Comparing tans was a big thing with The Faces.) Rod and Britt Ecklund got up to go back to the hotel, and when they got there, they were told that they were being evicted from their room. Helen Reddy and her manager husband Jeff Wald had just blown into town and demanded their usual room, which was occupied by Rod and Britt. Coward that I am, I stayed on the beach, sipping piña coladas. But when Mac—Ian McLagan—got wind of it, he went running up to the hotel cursing. He punched Helen Reddy's husband, knocking him against a wall, and a big painting of John Constable's "Haywain" fell right on his head. It was like a scene from a cartoon. Nevertheless, the hotel management didn't change its mind. Rod had to get out. But we made them suffer for it.

While Rod and Britt were packing, we stopped up the toilets so they would flood as soon as you flushed them. We put booby traps above the doors, sawed the legs off the bed and put them back under it, and clogged up the mouthpiece of the phone so no one could hear the person calling out. I wish I had been there to see them walk in the door and have things fall on their heads. Then, flush the toilet and have the bathroom flood. And finally, sit on the bed to complain to reception, only to have their bed collapse while they scream their lungs out over the phone without being heard.

We also played pranks like that on people we liked. Our manager Billy Gaff was frequently a victim. We'd invade his

room in the middle of the night while he was asleep. We'd get the keys from reception and burst into his room all at once, yelling our heads off. We'd turn his bed over on top of him, pull his pants off, flood the bathtub, and disconnect all the lights. So he'd be crawling around in the pitch dark, shouting, "If you don't (crash!) stop this right now (kerplunk!), I refuse to carry on working for you (boing!)." In the course of it all, we'd naturally empty his room of furniture. That'd go out the window, as simple as that. And with his mattress on the front lawn, the lights unplugged, and an inch of water on the floor, we'd charge out of the room with as much gusto as when we charged in.

But Billy Gaff was a great guy. He went to bat for us a lot. I remember around '70 we played a big festival in the Pocono Mountains. The whole thing was draggin' out. Everyone wanted to do their show and leave. Backstage, ELP's manager, Dee Anthony, was strangling Billy Gaff about whose group would go on first and when. All the other managers were pushing each other against walls. Well, we were one of the last bands to go on—at dawn! There was dew all over the place. After our set we left in the last helicopter that Three Dog Night were about to board. As we were lifting off—they yelled, "Wait for us!" But we flew away, sticking out our tongues at them, and laughing. Danny, their singer, still jokes about it.

Although Keith Moon was famous for turning into an art form the craft of hotel demolition, The Faces pioneered it. In certain midwest towns, we'd get incredibly bored, no one to call, nothing to do, everything closed. We just had to create our own fun, which is how rock 'n' roll destruction has come about. We were barred from so many hotels—the entire Holiday Inn chain—that we had to check in as Fleetwood Mac lots of times. (Got *them* some good press. Not to mention lawsuits, I suppose.)

Sometimes we'd have parties where we'd round up tons of people—even strangers—just to see how many people we could fit into one room. Naturally, at least one person would be in a drunken stupor, fall over, and set a whole thing off, with people toppling over like dominoes. In fact, a guy once literally went through the door, leaving behind, seemingly, the shape of his body—like in a comic book or cartoon.

Revenge, not just fun, was also the motivation for a lot of the

stuff we did. Room service in Sweden once charged us the equivalent of a hundred dollars for a fuckin' tiny plate of cheese. So before we left, we got our roadie to bring up a hacksaw. We sawed through the legs of all the chairs and put them back together, so that if someone sat down, they'd risk crashing to the floor, and possibly through the ceiling of the room below.

Another time, in Europe, the hotel refused to give us the extra suite we asked for. So we created one by taking all the furniture out of our rooms and arranging it in the corridor. We hammered up the pictures, making a replica of our rooms. Anyone expecting to walk down the usual boring hallway actually wound up walking into someone's room. It really threw people. Especially because we just acted natural, reading magazines, carrying on conversations as if we were relaxing in our own suite. When the hotel manager got off the elevator he nearly went into cardiac arrest, but he did smile and say it had better not be there when he got back.

Our strangest stay was in Germany. The place must've been run by former members of the Gestapo. We came in from an early concert there, and everyone piled into my room about 10 P.M. We heard loud footsteps coming down the corridor. Someone stopped outside and yelled, "You vill go to sleep now!" We laughed our heads off, thinking it was a prank. Then we heard it again. "You vill go to sleep! Now!" Next thing we knew, the electricity in the room was shut off. We wound up crawling out the window to carry on our little party for a few more hours. But in the morning we were all woken up at eight o'clock by the same voice. This time he was shouting, "You vill vake up now!"

Hotels weren't our only prey, though. One time, Rod and I went down to the docks, untied a couple boats, and let them drift downstream. It was almost like that Marx Brothers scene from *At the Circus,* with the orchestra frantically playing, not realizing they're floating off somewhere. The only thing missing was the orchestra.

I also remember Rod's fascination with trains back then. And in Tucson, we had the chance to derail one. Well, wait. It was a mini-train. I mean, it was a train that was like one of those rides at an amusement park. Big enough for little kids to get in, for trips around the hotel grounds where we were. It was late at night, no kids were on it. We fucked around with the tracks, got it going, and next thing you know, whoop! Right off the tracks, tumbling down a hill, with all the cars toppling and crumbling on one another. We made like that Monty Python scene: "Run away!"

In Washington, D.C., we got to play with the real thing. A real live locomotive train. Me and Rod were reading menus in a restaurant, and saw this big train sittin' out back. We hopped aboard and, after looking around a few minutes, proceeded to release the brakes. The thing started moving and we jumped off yelling, zoomed back into the restaurant, we hid in there while this giant conductor-less locomotive rolled off into the sunset.

The reason we were in Washington was to do a gig with Janis Joplin. She was with Big Brother & The Holding Co. It was an afternoon show. Everyone woke up moments before going onstage, but both bands played great. The only problem was that Janis had her eyes on me. She even sent her big guitar player to come and get me. "Janis wants to see you," he said. "Can't you get me out of it?" I begged him. She used to drink Southern Comfort non-stop, and had a complexion like a boy in puberty. I mean, she was a very sweet lady, I'm sure, but she just didn't, um, move me. Somehow, I escaped her clutches, but god, she coulda put me through a wall!

That reminds me of the time we were in London doing the "Top of the Pops" TV show. Gladys Knight was on the same episode. We lifted Mac up, opened the door to her dressing room, yelled "He loves you!" and dropped him in. We slammed the door and ran away. He wound up staying in there for over an hour. Don't get the wrong idea—even though he did come out threatening to join the Pips.

We once got Ronnie Lane to French kiss a cabdriver. It was somewhere in Sweden. Half the fun was the language barrier. We were riding from the airport to the hotel, and Ronnie had to sit up front next to the driver. We kept teasing the guy, "Oh, he loves you, he loves you." He barely understood it, and was sort of smiling awkwardly. We started yelling, "C'mon, Ronnie, show him! Show him!" Finally, Ronnie lunged over and stuck his tongue in the guy's mouth. We rolled on the floor laughing.

BOBBY WOMACK

I adore Bobby. He's a true friend of mine. And I'm a true fan of his. He never met with the worldwide commercial success he deserved, but the man is a legend. He played with Sam Cooke and many of the greats. Bobby wrote "It's All Over Now," but The Stones covered it and had a bigger hit with it than he did. A few years later, The Faces also did that song. And since we did a lot of Sam Cooke songs, too, Bobby was kinda itchy to check The Faces out. He came to see us in Detroit in '72. He thought I was Rod. But he quickly learned the difference. Rod was in such awe of him that he had a reverse reaction, acting kind of nasty to him. Womack pulled me aside and said, "The way things are going, I wish *you* were the Rod I thought I was gonna meet." Bobby and I hit it off right away. We never lost contact. He said, "Whenever you want me, I'll be there." And he was true to his word. He helped me a lot on my solo albums, and then me and Keith called him in to help on the "Dirty Work" album. He, in turn, brought Don Covay, another r&b legend, into the studio with us. It was great to

have people with their experience to bounce ideas off. And you can hear their stamp all over "Dirty Work."

I suppose we were just as reckless onstage as we were off. We never went through any painstaking rehearsals. If something didn't sound right, we just figured, screw it, it'll come together once we're onstage. One of the most embarrassing moments I ever had in public was with The Faces. It was at Madison Square Garden, just as the band was being announced. My roadie Chuch Magee hands me my guitar. The lights are down, we're heading toward the stage, and we have to plow our way through all these backstage people, to go up the stairs and come out from behind the amps. What I didn't realize was that my tuning pegs got bashed around by everybody. The lights go on—"Ladies and gentlemen, The Faces!"—and it's my cue to start the show with this big chord. Kroing!! It was the worst note I ever heard. I gingerly went up to the mike: "Um, just talk amongst yourselves for a few minutes." It was supposed to be "Stay with Me," but "Stuck with It" was a better description. Twenty thousand people watched me tune my guitar while Rod paced around the stage. It was very unnerving. I didn't feel right the whole show.

It was great when all of us guys got together for a reunion at Wembley in July, '86. After all the shit we'd been through individually, and after eleven years since we played as a group, we still had that carefree attitude—"We'll wing it." Rod came in and said, "Instead of rehearsing, let's go 'round to the pub." We all said, "Yeah!" Just like the old days. Who are we to fuck with tradition?

We reminisced about lots of things. Pretty nostalgic. Bill Wyman volunteered to play bass, which was the one thing that stood out as being different. Ronnie Lane was singing great, but it's hard for him to play guitar, so Bill had to sit in. Ronnie still retained his sense of humor. MTV was poking its cameras in our faces backstage, and he told this great joke I knew wouldn't get on the air: "Two midgets go up to a nunnery, knock on the door, and ask to see the Mother Superior. She comes out, and one of the midgets asks, 'Do you have any midget nuns here?' She says, 'Good Heavens, no, we don't.' So the midget thinks a minute, then asks her, 'Well, do you have *any* midget nuns in *any* of the nunneries around here?' 'No, no,' she answers him, 'Heavens, no.' So the other midget nudges the first one, and goes, 'See, I told you you fucked a penguin.'"

I always kept a close eye on The Stones. First off, I was a real fan. But more importantly, I knew I was destined to become one of them. I knew it from the start. Honest. I was really excited by them when I saw their earliest publicity shots, them standing by the Thames with their long scraggly hair blowing in the wind. I sort of looked up to them because they were a few years older than me. (They still are!) Before they actually became The Rolling Stones, they were each individually playing on the same club circuit as my older brothers, with guys like Alexis Korner. In the early sixties, *every*body seems to have played with Alexis at some point. Charlie Watts wound up playing in the same band as my oldest brother, Art. So Art used to see Charlie all the time. He remembers how his father would take his drums around. Mr. Watts would help Charlie load and unload the drums from the back of a van, and help him set up. It went on briefly even after Charlie joined The Stones.

The first time I saw The Stones live as a group was at the Richmond Jazz Festival in, I think, '64. They were playing inside a tent that was bopping up and down. It looked like an elephant, with its ass rockin' and rollin' from side to side. From outside, you could tell something good was happening in there. I went in and stood at the back. I was an awkward 17-year-old, totally intrigued by it all. I remember being the last one to leave. Walking out, as I kept watching The Stones hauling their equipment off the stage without looking where I was going, I smashed my leg against a pole that held the tent up.

The next time I saw them was at Windsor Cavern. They were

working pretty hard, doing two shows a day in separate places, not making much money, still having to wear uniforms. But they were pretty popular locally, so there was this long line of people waiting to get in, zigzagging up and down and across the streets. Windsor's a bit like San Francisco, with all the hills. Anyway, everyone assumed that The Stones were already backstage tuning up. Instead, this putrid orange van pulls up, packed airtight with amps and human cattle. The driver—it must have been Stu—gets out, walks to the back door of the van, and opens it. Pouring out like a broken dam come five guys, falling into the gutter with their wrinkled uniforms, sprawling around in the dirt.

Yes, even then I knew I belonged in that band. I've always been such a believer in fate that I just counted on it happening. I figured I'd be patient with it, go about my business for several years, and that it would certainly fall into my lap someday. I just had to wait it out. And I did. Over ten years.

The strange thing that few people know is that I could've—and would've—joined The Stones a lot earlier than I did. It was in '69, about the time Brian Jones died. Ian Stewart phoned up the studio where The Small Faces were rehearsing and got Ronnie Lane on the line. "Now that Brian's gone," Stu told him, "do you think Woody would be happy with the job?" If *I* had answered the phone (I was in the other fuckin' room!) I would've said, "Is sixty seconds too late to show up?" But Ronnie Lane, fully aware of that fact, answered, "No thanks, I think he's quite happy where he is." It wasn't until five or so years later that I found out this story, and by then, I *was* a fuckin' Rolling Stone!

Two days after Brian died, The Stones played Hyde Park, which is where they introduced Mick Taylor as their new guitarist. The funny thing is that I coincidentally bumped into Jagger and Watts on their way to the show. "Have a good gig," I told them, ignorant of the fact that it could've been *me* up there with 'em.

Mick Taylor was in The Stones from '69 to '74. I was there in '74 when he left the group, although I didn't realize it at first. It was at a party for Clapton at Robert Stigwood's house. I rode there in a car with both Micks and Marshall Chess, the president of Rolling Stones Records. Mick Taylor was talking very quietly with Marshall. When Mick Taylor cut out from the party really early, I assumed he got ill or something. In actuality, he just finished telling Mick he was quitting the band. I didn't find that out for months, though. Because Mick comes walking up to me, beating around the bush, sending out all these feelers. "Let's say Mick Taylor left the band. If it became possible for you to join The Stones, would you?" And I said, "Sure, but I've got The Faces, you know, and I'd never want to mess that up. I love those guys; they're great friends." Mick understood. "Oh, no," he went, "I wouldn't want you to split up The Faces. But if you can work it out, it'd be great, huh?" So I told him. "Look, if you ever get desperate, give me a call." A few months later, the phone rings, and it's Mick: "I'm desperate." Luckily, within a day or two—and this is how fate has always played such a large role in my life—Rod said, "I'm quitting The Faces." A golden opportunity. I didn't have to break any news to the boys. The Faces were folding.

The Faces played two final tours in '75, even though we all knew it was over. In fact, on the last tour—after I already did my first tour with The Stones—the posters read "Faces 1975 Fall Tour," but we'd scribble on them, "Faces 1975 Downfall Tour."

I joined The Stones in '75 when they held auditions in Germany while recording "Black and Blue." They put up a whole bunch of guitarists at the Munich Hilton. I had a room in between Beck and Harvey Mandel, who's a great session musician. Nils Lofgren also wanted to join. So Keith said to him, "Oh, yeah, how much you gonna pay me to get an audition?" I respect him now, but at that time, Nils was in no position to invite himself anywhere. I remember him from awhile before

that. He was this tiny, spotty kid that would show up in dressing rooms everywhere, wielding a guitar and hoping for a chance to play. "Get this fuckin' kid outta here!" everyone would yell about him. But that scrawny little kid wouldn't leave. "Look, I can play," he'd yell. He once popped into The Faces' dressing room in Washington, D.C., with his usual rap. We picked him up and dropped him into Janis Joplin's dressing room next door. (Maybe *she* turned him into a MAN!) But I admire the guy's perseverence. He's great today, doin' real well with Bruce "Stringbean."

Clapton also auditioned for The Stones at the same time. He could have cut it. In fact, I still get ribbed by him to this day. "I could've had that job," he'll say. And I answer, "No you couldn't. You haven't got the personality."

Even before those auditions, the cards were stacked in my favor. My link to The Stones was pretty strong. Keith had already helped me on my first solo album. It was sheer luck, really. My ex-wife, Krissie, was down at a club and saw Keith at another table. She could tell he wanted to get away from the people he was with, so she went up to him and said, "Hey, wanna come back and hear what Woody's done for his solo album?" Keith jumped at the chance to leave the club. He came over to my house, expecting to stay a few hours. He wound up staying four months. Then we did a concert together. It was my first-ever solo album. It's what gave me the itch to put The New Barbarians together five years later.

I was also very close with Mick on a social level right before I joined the band. We hung out with each other on the west coast a lot. He and I once went to Ireland together, where we spent days writing songs on the Guinness estate in Dublin. Just out in the fields, near these old ruins. He helped me out a lot. Then I helped *him* record a demo of "It's Only Rock 'N' Roll." At the same time we recorded "I Can Feel the Fire" for my first solo album. It was at my house, the Wick, in Surrey, England. We fooled around with it a few times, then decided to get it on tape. I had a few friends over. We wound up with Kenney Jones on drums, Willie Weeks on bass, me and Mick on acoustic guitars, and Bowie sang backing vocals. The basic track remained pretty much the same so there I was, contributing to a Stones album before I was even a Stone.

But the affinity between me and The Stones came mostly

from the Faces–Stones rivalry. If The Stones had a funny, sarcastic rapport with The Beatles in the sixties, then it was The Faces who they had that with in the seventies. It was really funny, all the digs that went back and forth.

Although we'd never admit it, The Faces were actually pretty influenced by those old farts The Stones. We sometimes warmed up in the dressing room by listening to the "Get Yer Ya Ya's Out" album. Mick definitely had an effect on Rod. Mick's running joke—and it was true—was, "I see Rod's wearing the same pajamas this year that I wore last year." The feather boa, the cheesecloth outfits, Mick was right. It didn't even look good on Rod most of the time. It all came to a head when Mick came to see The Faces play at Roosevelt Stadium in Newark, New Jersey. Mick was standing behind an amp and he kept yelling at me, "Look at the LV!" ("LV" being lead vocalist, an acronym I helped initiate.) He was making funny faces at Rod, but I didn't even defend my own LV. I just held my hands up in the air with a dumb look on my face: "I know. What can I do?" Mick and I had this hilarious exchange going the whole night.

You see, usually those digs came to us second hand. The Stones each sent jokes and insults back and forth by the use of, er, messengers. Since both groups were on the road a lot, we wouldn't get to see each other too often. So groupies would be the ones to pass messages (and probably diseases) from one band to the other. (Mind you, that was back in the days when you could catch a disease and get rid of it as quickly as you caught it. Back in the days when men were men and sheep were nervous.)

Seventy-two was a big tour year for both bands. We were never in the same city at the same time, but we'd often follow one another into town a few days apart. Mick would send out hints to the girls while he was onstage. He'd make a triangle with his fingers, for instance, and then all the local groupies would know he was staying at the Triangle Inn. Anyway, as he'd be finishing up with these chicks, zippin' his fly, the girls would say, "Oh, do you have any messages for Rod or Woody? We're gonna see them on Friday." Or vice versa. Another method of communication the two bands used was carving messages on the walls of our dressing room when we knew the other band would be playing the same hall.

When The Stones and Faces did finally meet up, it was in L.A. at the Beverly Wilshire. It was the first and last time The Stones and Faces ever stayed at the same hotel. Naturally, my room was the place everyone gathered. All the Faces, all the Stones, all the managers, roadies, groupies, etc. The trouble was, the room had mirrors, everywhere. And of course, not a single one was left intact. I've never been allowed back there. But at least I have about seventy-seven years of bad luck to look forward to!

DAVID BOWIE

He's such a down-to-earth, lovely, talented guy. A long-time pal. When I was in the Jeff Beck Group, he lived right down the block from me. We'd hang out and listen to records together. I always thought he was a real character, wearing those floppy hats back then. That was before he got well known. Before he fell to earth.

He recently rang me up in New York from Switzerland to wish me a "happy birthday." That was real nice of him.

Jo and I saw him play at Madison Square Garden in '83. Tina Turner was also backstage. He had an intermission during his show, so he came offstage, and there I was, waiting for him. I hit him with, "Hey, you got that five dollars you owe me!" It was just a joke, and I really didn't expect a response. With all the crazi-ness backstage, he could've ignored it and gone off to worry about his makeup. Instead, he didn't miss a step. He played along: "Sorry, Ronnie, I left it in my other pants." He stayed and talked with me and Tina, asked Jo how she was coming along—she was pregnant with Tyrone—while all his people were bitching at him to get back onstage. "No," he said, "I just wanna stay here and hang out with my friends." He's so funny.

But I've seen him go through some miserable times, too. I've helped him through a few traumas. One time, he called me up, saying that all these strange people were partying in his house and he couldn't get rid of them. "You gotta get me outta this house," he urged me. So I rode over there with Fred Sessler and found him huddled in the corner, shivering, in pieces. So we took him away and brightened him up.

Once, when I was staying with The Faces at the Beverly Wilshire Hotel, there was a knock on my door. I open it up and it's David. He falls forward into my arms, with tears coming out of his eyes like Olive Oyl. "He ripped me off!" he was yelling. It was about his manager. "After all these years, he fucking turns around to rip me off!" He was really let down, but I talked him through it.

My first public appearance with The Stones was on the back of a flatbed truck, riding down Fifth Avenue in New York. It was publicity to announce the '75 tour. The Stones' p.r. guy got all these press people to cram into the dining room of a fancy hotel. They must've thought Mick would go through a whole bit. Instead, that comedian Professor Irwin Corey began babbling on. Just as all these journalists are going "What the fuck?" The Stones come rolling up outside the hotel playing "Brown Sugar" on the back of the truck. It was great to see these guys with their cameras and microphones rushing out of that hotel, clamoring and running alongside. I was carrying on conversations with the New York cops. "Hey," they were askin' me, "you gonna get us tickets? We couldn't get in to see The Faces."

We created a traffic jam. People are trying to get to work carrying their briefcases and all of a sudden, The Rolling Stones come driving down their block. I told Keith, "They probably think someone slipped acid in their coffee this morning."

A few weeks later, the tour started, and I played my first show as a Stone, on my birthday. Not a bad birthday gift for a kid who always dreamed of bein' in The Stones. That first show, in Baton Rouge, Louisiana, was a crash course for me. I mean, I knew most of The Stones' songs, but had never actually played them. I had to channel the intricacies of around 150 songs from my head through my fingers. And I soon learned that I had to be on guard against Mick pulling the rug from under my feet. He would jokingly physically attack me onstage, as a means of keeping me on my toes, I suppose. But it reached

the point where Charlie stopped a few rehearsals right in the middle of a song: "You don't hit my friend Woody!" But Mick needed someone like me to fool around with. He never had that chance with the inanimate Bill Wyman or the others. Mick Taylor just wasn't that kind of guy either. Jagger wouldn't dare fuck with Keith. And Charlie had the drums to protect him. Otherwise, there would have been lots of cat-and-mouse chases onstage through the years.

The only shitty thing Mick did to me was when he tongue kissed me on national TV. It was on "Saturday Night Live," just after we finished the '78 tour. There we were onstage, doing "Beast of Burden," I think, and I had my eyes closed for a few seconds and suddenly, I feel this wet warm thing slurping on my face. It was Mick's tongue. I tried to kick him, but he was too fast. He loves putting people on the spot—even in front of an entire nation of TV viewers. I really didn't mind too much, but it didn't sit well with my mother-in-law. She got very upset by it and I was embarrassed as hell the next time I saw her.

We all had our share of embarrassment on that show, because one by one our voices went. (Even John Belushi's.) I was the first to lose my voice during rehearsals on Wednesday. Mick and Keith were both laughing at me. Then Keith lost his voice —and that left one less person laughing. Finally, with hours to go before airtime, the LV himself, Mick, came down with it too. As we went on, I was spraying the whole studio with Chloraseptic. Bill had a good chuckle over it.

But a few weeks earlier, we were in St. Paul, Minnesota. As we were leaving the stage, Bill waved to his many fans and then leaned against a curtain, thinking there was a wall behind it. There wasn't. He toppled five hundred feet or so, knocking himself unconscious. Everyone in the band had left the arena. Keith and I were already sitting in our limo, ready to leave. We thought Bill had come out with us and was sitting in the limo ahead. Our driver was honking at Bill's driver to roll out of the place. Little did he realize that poor Bill was sprawled out on some sticky floor inside.

Such are the rises and falls of The Rolling Stones. One time in Frankfurt, Keith slipped on—what else—a frankfurter someone had thrown onstage. It was hilarious—more like the Flintstones than The Rolling Stones. Next thing I know, I turn around and Keith's flat on his ass. We all laughed and pointed at him.

That's one of the few times we've had a meal thrown onstage. Believe me, we get lots of things. Of course, there's the common bras and panties. That's not unusual—I then spend a good part of the show scanning the audience for the girl with the missing drawers. In California, we once got bombarded by shoes. A couple of girls threw up their sneakers. They nearly hit Mick, so he went up to the mike half annoyed, half kidding: "Okay, why don't you all throw up your shoes at once and get it over with." Next thing we know, it's raining shoes and sandals, and we're all running around the stage, trying not to get hit. There were millions of 'em. One guy threw up this great cowboy boot. After the show we were scurrying around looking for the other one, but we couldn't find it. We had an agreement that whoever found it would keep the pair.

A few times, I had to beg people to throw things *back* at me. At one show, I grabbed a hat off the piano and tossed it into the crowd. Then I look over and see Mick giving me dirty looks. I didn't realize it was his hat, which he paid a ton of money for. His favorite hat. So I leaned over the stage to plead with the guy to give it back. He was about ten feet away, so he passed it down through a chain of people and I finally got it back. As a consolation, I passed the guy my Jack Daniels on the rocks.

At another show, I was wearing this ring my mother-in-law gave me. It was a little too big for my finger. When I was gesturing to the crowd, it just flew off into the audience. My heart pounded. It had a lot of sentimental value. So I went up to the mike—right in the middle of a song—and said, "My mother-in-law will kill me if I don't get that ring back." Two minutes later, Whoop! It comes skydiving back onto the stage. That was such a great feeling. You usually don't get things like that back.

I do sometimes worry about certain dangerous elements being tossed up onstage. A bottle once missed Charlie and me by inches. The guy threw it just to attract attention, though. Maybe he was a jealous boyfriend!

The last time we played Nice, France, the phony Hell's Angels were there, and there was a big commotion in the crowd. Throngs of people were surging. From where I was standing, it was pretty scary. Finally, Jim Callahan's super-tough security strongmen, swung into action, perhaps preventing another potential Altamont by cracking the key troublemaker's bones.

In '81, we did a show on Keith's birthday in Virginia. During the encore, "Satisfaction," while all the balloons and streamers were coming down, out of the confusion, some guy came running down a ramp straight towards Keith. I dunno, he was probably a kid who just wanted to shake Keith's hand, maybe wish him a happy birthday. But, you never know . . . At any rate, Keith unstrapped his guitar, delivered a stiff blow to the guy's head and carried on playing without missing a note. My immediate reaction was, "Hey, Keith, he's only a fan. No reason to fuckin' hit him." And Keith went, "Oh, yeah, what if he had a fuckin' gun in his hand, or a knife." Um, okay, I suppose Keith was right.

You see, Lennon was hit the year before, so everyone was reasonably tense. Mick beefed up his security, and he's kept it up to this day. Even when he's not on tour. He would come over to my house in New York and I'd have to escort him back home in the middle of the night. "Woody, will you please walk

me back home?" Mind you, the guy lived three short blocks away from me. (And then I'd think, who's gonna walk *me* home from *his* house?) I bet he probably walks through Central Park dressed as a broom salesman.

For the most part, we've got some wonderful fans. They'll endure anything. We once played the Cotton Bowl in Dallas during a torrential rainstorm. Eighty thousand people were packed in there, absolutely drenched. Their homes were probably floating away a few miles down the road, but those folks stayed out there for the duration. We felt so appreciative that we kept walking to the front of the stage from underneath the shelter we had, trying to get as wet as they were. We had those wireless remote amps, so we were able to do it without getting electrocuted. And hey, even if we *could've* gotten electrocuted, anything for our fans, right?

We've got this one fan, a girl in a wheelchair, who travels everywhere to see us. She's legally blind, too, with these humongous glasses. (Come to think of it, that's probably why Keith is her favorite!) It's nice to see that concert promoters set up special sections for people in wheelchairs. My dad was probably the most inebriated of them all! Hmm, that reminds me. Lennon had all these vicious cripple jokes. You know him, such a wonderful sick sense of humor. But the fact is, if he had been a cripple, he'd have joked the piss out of himself too.

By the time I joined The Stones in the mid-seventies, the whole hotel-wrecking era had cooled off. Of course, no one told that to Keith Moon. For the most part, though, The Stones and I had gotten it out of our systems by then. And now we're a little more mature, with our own families and responsibilities. Oh, sure, there's the occasional TV in the flower bed, but overall, hotels welcome our patronage with open arms. I don't think we have to register as Fleetwood Mac anymore. Well, actually, come to think of it, there is one hotel in New York that Keith and I have an ongoing thing with. They say I owe them $4,000. Even if I remembered which hotel it was, I wouldn't mention it here. No need to remind their accounting department. It's been about ten years since we stayed there. Keith kept hanging out in my room, awake for two days straight, jamming and pacing around. The hotel claims that we literally wore out a brand new carpet in just two days' time. I refused to pay for it all. I wanted Keith to pay half, but naturally he said, "No fucking way."

I suppose we progressed from breaking walls to just ruining carpets. On another tour, we snuck into our promoter, Paul Dainty's room, and stuffed it with dozens of live pigeons. The carpet, the furniture, everything—completely plastered in pigeon shit. I wound up drawing the picture on this page with a slight exaggeration on the theme—filling his room with horses. Hmmm, remember that one for next time.

When we were in Europe in '82, we were causing a big commotion partying in one of our rooms after a show. It was pretty wild. Suddenly, there was a knock on the door. "Open up, this is the police!" Holy shit! I started to imagine the next day's headlines. People start scrambling all around the room, looking for their clothes, flushing things down the toilet, running around like chickens with their heads cut off. I took a deep breath and opened the door . . . and in walked fuckin' Sting, Andy Summers, and Stewart Copeland.

Getting up onstage is the fruit of my labor. After spending months locked in a studio, that's what I look forward to. There's no other place to get such immediate feedback, such a rapport with your fans. You certainly can't achieve that with a recording. I was born to play live. I love life on the road.

After a while all the cities start to look the same, with a few exceptions. You know you're in Dublin when all you see is green. You know you're in L.A. when all you see is sun and smog. Occasionally, there'll be something that makes a specific show or city stick out in your mind. But it wouldn't be fair or accurate to say that there's one hall or city we always play best in, or worst in. However, I do remember one show we did in a bull ring in Barcelona. I played incredibly well that night. It's a totally selfish and subjective thing. The others may not remember it at all.

No matter where we are, though, there's a few things that are always the same. Like the unbelievable amount of adrenaline you get. One time, I had so much energy, I couldn't resist jumping on Mick's back, right in the middle of a song. He didn't know what the hell was going on. His first instinct was to flip me over. It was like a scene from a bad kung fu movie. The stage was on an incline so I rolled really fast. But I was successful in keeping my guitar from hitting the ground and getting knocked out of tune. I'm proud of that.

That high energy level sticks with you after you get offstage. I can't get to sleep for hours. Before the show, there's an incredible amount of nervous excitement. Everyone's pacing around.

The tune-up room is the psychotherapy area for the guitarists to get their shit together and loosen up. It can get pretty funny in there. Keith and I always take the attitude that when we unplug ourselves in the tuning room and go out there, we should try to keep that same private laugh, but with 50,000 people watching.

Believe it or not, Bill Wyman's usually back there playing table tennis before a show. Nothing like a game of Ping Pong minutes before you go on. Actually, he's quite good. Beats me every time, without even moving around. He stands in one place and lets his hands do all the work. A very economic use of the floor. As for Mick, he'll pop into the tuning room and sing a few numbers with us, something like "Angie," even if we're not doing that song in the show. Charlie will be banging his knees with his sticks. Charlie's great. Always on one plane. He could be on his farm or in front of 100,000 people, and he'll act just the same.

As we're walking up the stairs to the stage, Bill will suddenly yell with concern, "Don't forget it's an E into an F." And he'll give you hell for it later if you fuck up. After the first couple songs are out of the way, we'll all breathe a sigh of relief, especially if we've settled into the pocket. We might wink at each other, or shake hands, or raise our glasses. Mick'll say, "Great, Woody," with a tinge of surprise in his voice. Of course, if it's *not* going well, Mick will have this sour expression on his face. And Keith will give you a look that says, "Your life has been a complete waste of sperm and egg."

All sorts of things can go wrong that are beyond our control. Like mechanical problems. Those are usually taken care of pretty quickly. It's some of the "people problems" onstage that are kind of hard to repair on the spot. On the '81 tour, in Kansas City, we heard that Mick Taylor was in town and we invited him up onstage for a few numbers.

Perhaps the reunion overexcited him. He seemed to refuse to realize how much the band had changed since his departure. He shocked us with how loud he was blasting it. Bulldozing through parts of songs that should have been subtle, ignoring breaks and taking uninvited solos. And the volume! I thought me and Keith play loud, but he was easily three times louder than us. I was standing next to him, passing along messages from Keith who would say, "Tell that fucker to turn it down!" I was a little more diplomatic: 'Um, Mick, the song is finished." Or "It's in E, not F." Afterwards, Keith told me, "It's a good thing you were standing in between us or I'd have flattened him." But he's a lovely man, and it was great to see him.

I have a great deal of respect for him. In fact, my job in The Stones wasn't even the first time I filled his shoes. He and I go way back. I was playing a show in '65 with my first band, The Birds, at an army base. Mick Taylor was in The Gods who were on the same bill. But he was so nervous that I played in his band instead of him. He asked me to. Those army guys were a

tough audience. They didn't warm up no matter what. By the end of the show, the place—a dark gym—was completely empty. I bring up that whole story because I want to make it clear that I think he's a nice guy and there was never any rivalry between him and me.

Elton John did a similar thing in '75. He came on, invited, for "Honky Tonk Woman," but never got off Billy Preston's piano. Billy was standing there, incredibly pissed off, trying to nudge his way back onto the piano stool. But Elton didn't give up until the show was over!

I've become something of a mediator with The Stones. I guess that, having joined last, I'm able to be objective, and to complement each member. Sort of play the Henry Kissinger role. Maybe I should be in politics. Reagan, Gorbachev, and Wood.

Seriously, I wish I could have had that Henry Kissinger impact on others, like the Beatles in '70. If I had been able to get to Brian Jones in time, I would've tried my hardest to repair him, too; as a fan of the band, I'd have loved to see him well. I wish I had gotten to Elvis when he was going down. I'd never have let him die. I would've gotten him away from those bodyguards and doctors. He just needed a pal, that's all. Ah, these are all fantasy situations, hindsight. And on today's scene, I don't think there's anyone worth saving!

I do take a lot of credit for The Stones' survival. In a recent TV interview, Bill Wyman said, "The reason the band is still together is sitting right next to me," and he nudged me in the ribs, on camera. He said that he really lost interest during The Stones' lull in the mid-seventies, but that my arrival rejuvenated everyone. I agree. I know I gave those guys a kick in the pants. I became someone Mick could bounce off onstage—figuratively and literally! And I gave the whole unit an objective ear to sound ideas off.

But it's only now that I can pat myself on the back for that. For ten years I felt like an apprentice. I was the youngest and the latest to arrive. I had to swallow my pride—especially in business matters—because I wasn't there from the beginning. I accepted being the brunt of a lot of jokes. It's finally worn off, but I wasted too much time thinking about it.

Keith always reminds me that I've been in The Stones longer

than either Mick Taylor or Brian Jones. I feel great about that. My new self-confidence makes me realize that talent is the reason I'm in this great band. And it allows me to feel free about having a role in decision-making, even if it's just as mediator. Other than guitar playing, someone like Mick Taylor had no input in the band. I'm different—I wouldn't be fulfilled as a backup musician. Of course, I do play second or third fiddle in The Stones. But I don't mind that, 'cuz I still make my impression felt.

That's not to say I don't have to swallow my pride now and then and shut up. But so do Charlie and Bill. Everybody has his role, and it's a checks-and-balances thing. I mean, there were times when Mick suggested Bill leave the band. He probably did the same thing about me. Maybe some of us *are* expendable. Yet, obviously we're all still here. No one person can run away with things, whether it be Mick or Keith or anyone. Me, Bill, and Charlie have a collective weight that helps determine the band's future. Even Keith's admitted that he and Mick cancel each other out, leaving us. Keith says he can't get divorced, that he and Mick are like Siamese twins, but some of the problems can be operated on by Doctors Wood, Wyman, and Watts.

I don't always give my opinions publicly, but I do air my gripes with the other four guys. The release of the "Dirty Work" album was a very frustrating time, and I let them know it. The bone of contention, of course, was Mick's reluctance to tour. The album was selling pretty well, and a Stones tour would have done wonders for it. Sitting around the fuckin' house when we should be out on the road really sucks. And the lost income is a tough thing for me to waive.

Mick and Keith can argue about touring or whatever until the cows come home. They're secure financially. They're content with the accomplishments they've made at their ages. But I'm younger. I've still got loads of things to do. I sympathize with Mick to an extent, especially about the physical strain a tour puts on him. That's why it's time we got a small stage, and just played some kick-ass rock 'n' roll, without all the exhausting theatrics. Yet I suppose I understand his not wanting to do that. It's fine, he could have his reign for a bit.

I only want to know the boundaries in which I have to work. When I saw the layoff coming, in the spring of '86, I started getting busy with loads of other people: Don Johnson, Chuck Berry, Jerry Lee Lewis, Fats Domino, Ray Charles, and Carl Perkins. I just gotta get out there. But I'd have dropped all those things in a second for a Stones tour.

Charlie said to me, "The worst part of being a Rolling Stone is that out of twenty-five years, it's been five years of work, and twenty years of sitting on our fucking asses." I agree. The ratio's been even worse since I've been with 'em.

Where do I see The Stones in ten years? Doing reunions. Even if we didn't play from now until then, I think we'd have no problem fading in and out whenever we wanted. Maturity and geography may separate us for long periods of time, but we'd never break it all off. No matter how tense things could get, there'd never be a split like The Beatles'. Animosity will not be the factor that breaks up The Rolling Stones.

I look to the other Stones as brothers. Each of us does. Recently, though, it's been as if your brothers were in the Army for a while, or something. I mean, we don't get to see each other too often anymore. It's rare that all five of us are together at once, even if we're recording an album. That's what it's like between relatives—even blood relatives—that you have. It's great when you get together with 'em, but if you saw 'em every day, you'd grow a little bored and start getting on each other's nerves.

Mick and Keith have known each other longer than they've known anybody else in the band, or even in their lives, apart from their mums and dads. So it's understandable that they can get so frustrated with one another, like any sibling rivalry. Jesus, they've known each other for fuckin' forty years, since the local schoolyard. Like brothers, we get involved in each other's personal lives, occasionally being thanked for the help, and occasionally being slapped with a "Fuck off, it's *my* business!" I think that's what makes The Stones different from any flash-in-the-pan group out there. We've seen each other go through every fuckin' high and low there is—personally, professionally, financially, biologically . . .

Actually, Bill Wyman hasn't changed all that much through the years. Not since I've known him, anyway. If anything, he's getting younger instead of older. More power to him. He was, after all, dating a one-year-old. No, seriously, I think she was seventeen or so, one third his age. Bill has a son who's in his twenties. Come to think of it, they can go on double dates. Y'know, the funny thing is that when The Stones first started, it was Bill who was married with a kid. He was the family man, while Mick, Keith, and Brian were wild bachelors with no responsibilities. Now, Mick, Keith, and I are family men, and Bill is out there being a lady-killer. He really has gone girl crazy in the last few years. A real stud. He's told me that girls are his drug. Some musicians find solace in coke, smack, or booze. For Bill, it's women. That's fairly productive. (Reproductive, if he's not careful.)

Charlie's wearing his age like all those great jazzers. He's aging the way Ellington did, Count Basie, too. Real grace, class. Even the way he dresses now. Speaking of which, have you ever seen him without his trousers? He's got these massive legs from all that drumming. Real powerful legs. Charlie's no slight person. Inside and out. He had to put up with some tough times recently in the family department. It's no secret to any of you British tabloid readers. It warranted front pages when his daughter got expelled for smoking a joint in school and when his wife admitted herself into a booze clinic. But they've come out great. Charlie's real proud of his wife for realizing she had a problem and taking care of it. He was under a lot of strain for a while, but he'd let it out by coming into the studio and pounding the shit out of the drums. He's such a class act. A real inspiration to play with. When he's on, the whole band is on. Absolutely indispensable.

Keith's getting more distinguished-looking. Developed a handsome salt and pepper (and other condiments). He's no longer that spotty youth we all grew up with from Ed Sullivan or "Ready Steady Go." Now he's a salty old dog. As in my case, I think that his looks hint at the fact that he's been through a lot, yet I do think he's wearing his age and mileage quite well.

Mick's been looking great lately. Sometimes, he seems as young as when he first started out, despite comedians saying he now resembles Don Knotts. He's a hard one to catch on canvas, though. There's a lot of different sides to him, and when he flits so fast from one to the other, it gets a bit blurry. This one of him was how I saw him onstage in Philadelphia in '81. Pretty blurry. I called it "The Mustard Painting" because I used mustard for all the yellow.

I used to be a lot closer to Mick than I am now. That's mostly due to the fact that he's so involved with one woman, and with all of his kids. He is in serious danger of getting married. He's already pretty henpecked, actually. Then again, so am I. Wait, that's a bad word. I mean, it's creative henpecking. None of us are pussywhipped. I just have a conscientious lady who tries to get me doing what I should be doing. Going to sleep early, for instance. Keith gets a scolding when he stays out too late, but that usually happened when Patti was pregnant. Like I said, henpecking's a bad word. They're merely reminding us of our moral obligations, responsibilities. You've got to be sympathetic to a pregnant wife. If they want your company—pregnant or not—then your rowdy friends better be aware that they're getting thrown out. I used to get a lot of flack from Jerry

Hall for keeping Mick out late. Patti never hassled me, she'd just yell at Keith.

Of course, there are times when the band's needs are more important and immediate, and then the wives have to understand. Sometimes we can close ourselves off, like a bunch of guys in some dumb bikers' gang, and totally disregard the

women. Or disregard some of our male friends if they're only there to socialize. I mean, you'd never invite any good friend of yours to a private band rehearsal, 'cuz they'd just get the cold shoulder. It'd be embarrassing for the both of you. "We don't give a fuck if it's your *mother,*" the others would say, "we're here to rehearse, not socialize!"

In our line of work, there are so many people who take up your private time. I can understand the wives' frustrations. I'll have a full house of people over, jamming in the basement till all hours, thinking that that's normal. But it's really *ab*normal. You are supposed to have time for your family, your young kids. It's part of Keith's and my makeup. He's not happy unless he has a house bursting with rowdy people. He never wants 'em to leave. So you do need the guidance of a good woman, like my wife Jo, to keep a steady grasp on your health and on your everyday responsibilities. Fortunately for Bill Wyman, he's got several good women to keep a steady grasp on him!

IAN STEWART

Stu's absolutely irreplace-able. He was so well liked. No one had a bad word to say about him. We've all known many people who've died, but his death at the end of '85 touched the band more than anything else before. It was very sobering, especially since he led a real clean lifestyle. That was the irony, him always warning us not to burn the candle at both ends.

He was called the sixth Stone. But actually, he formed the band with Brian Jones. Chronologically, Stu was the *second* Stone. The two of them held auditions. Keith tried out,

and everyone went down there and got together. Stu was a featured member of the group until told to step into the background. He wasn't like the rest of The Stones—which was to his credit. But he played on just about every Stones album and at every Stones concert there ever was. He always had these critical comments about the band, opinions that would've earned anyone else a slap in the face. But Stu was always right, and it was constructive criticism. He'd always make faces when the band were "bad boys." "Who's gonna tell us off now?" Charlie said at the funeral.

We did a tribute show for him in early '86, with Beck,

Clapton, Townshend, Simon Kirke, and Jack Bruce all doing guest spots. It was at the 100 Club, a tiny place on Oxford Street in London. It was the first time in four years that The Stones played a concert together. Promoters had been waving millions of dollars in our faces to play, but there we were in a tiny club, playing Just for Stu. We knew that he must've been looking down at us, smiling, wondering why we all went to the trouble. The Stones would certainly be working as a unit for more if he were still with us to organize the band into action.

MARVIN GAYE

I love telling this one story about Marvin. Perhaps I'll call the story "Dead Singers' Dead Ringers." Oops, sorry 'bout that, Marvin. Man, could that guy sing! Well, anyway, me and Mick went to see Marvin's show a few years back in Jersey or Madison Square Garden, I don't remember. Not memorable for Mick and myself 'cuz we had no seats and were just running from side to side the whole show trying to catch a peek. We could hardly see a thing. But after the show, we all piled into Marvin's hotel room at the Plaza, with Linda Ronstadt and others. Mick and I went into the bedroom, where Marvin's brother was sitting on the bed wearing that hat. That woolly hat Marvin used to wear. So Mick unknowingly goes up to him and starts laying on all this advice, thinking he was Marvin. *Oh, you should have done this song, you should have done this, done that.* All that Jagger wisdom spewing forth, and then . . . "Hey, man, that's all well and good, but I'm Marvin's brother. Marvin will be back soon."

OTIS REDDING

I wish I had met him. But like so many great talents, he was taken from us too early. It's a little eerie that Steve Cropper, great session musician who played with Booker T & The MGs and The Blues Brothers, is still alive today simply because he missed the plane Otis was on.

I saw Otis play once in a London club called Blaise's, about '65. Just the other day Keith realized that he was there that exact same night with Brian Jones.

I suppose the trademark of a good singer or musician is that when you turn on the radio you immediately know who he is. That's Otis. Unmistakable voice. A class by himself. Keith's told me that one of the proudest moments of his career was when Otis covered "Satisfaction."

6

To me, being a rock star is just another label. It's like being a plumber. It's your identity and how you make your living. That's all. So many folks strive to become famous and quit their "day jobs." There's lots of things I wish *I* could do, but I simply can't. Being famous means that people see you as one thing for the rest of your life. A Rolling Stone forever. Of course, I'd rather be trapped here than anywhere else. It's self-inflicted. Besides, it's the same thing with any career you choose. If you're a doctor for twenty years, you're not likely to become a plumber, no matter how much you may want to. If I could be anything else, outside the entertainment business, I think I'd like to be an athlete. Lots of similarities. It's still a physical type of career, and possibly a public lifestyle, with lots of travel. I'd have loved to be a pro tennis player, or soccer player. Also, snooker, which is sort of like pool. In my old house, I had the table that belonged to Joe Davis, a former British champion. I played it constantly. It's a great game, very therapeutic. I also love basketball. I used to play the Americans at the U.S. Air Base when going to junior college.

Fame is a funny thing. When I was just starting out, I kidded myself that people knew who I was. But I had no proof for years. I was still in The Birds and was playing to 100 or 200 people a night. That's popular, but it wasn't fame. The proof didn't come until I was in the Jeff Beck Group and people would start complimenting my bass playing.

We put out some good records and got some airplay. But I tell you, to this day with The Stones, when I hear myself on the

radio, I'm sort of detached from it. Like I wasn't there behind it. I feel I was just part of the machine that generates a big noise, not realizing there are thousands of people in Radioland listening.

I've played in front of humongous crowds for almost twenty years. But that's a weird thing, too. I mean, in '75 I did two tours with The Faces and one with The Stones. I'm probably the only person to have played in front of two and a half million people in one year and still have them say, "Who is that guy?" But that's what I deserve for being a professional second banana. I'm the best at making others look good. I've done it my whole career. That's why my first solo album in '74 was appropriately titled "I've Got My Own Album to Do." My first big shot as a front man came in '79, when I took The New Barbarians on the road. Me doing lead vocals, playing guitar and some sax. Keith was on guitar, Mac on keyboards, Bobby Keys on sax, Ziggy Modeliste on drums, and Stanley Clarke on bass. I met Stanley Clarke in London one night at a club called Tramp's. He came up to me and told me how much he liked my bass playing on Beck's "Truth" album. Coming from him, that was a great compliment. And of course, it ingratiated him into being the bass player for The New Barbarians. It was easy to get Keith to back me up, because he wasn't doing anything else. "Hey, Keith." I rang him up. "You gonna sit on your ass for another few months or what?" Keith just said, "If you're touring, I'm on it." Actually, it was pretty convenient for him. Our first show helped him fulfill his commitment to the judge—he was ordered to do a benefit gig after his bust in Canada. So we played this concert for the blind (sure made our wardrobe selection easy), and then hit about fifteen U.S. cities in a month. Unfortunately, there were all these fans yelling, "Mick! Rod!" That was a bit of a blow to the ego. So much for "Front Man Ron Wood." In fact, when we did Milwaukee, the kids literally tore up the place when no surprise guests came on. We got slapped with a lawsuit. But I never promised any surprise guests. Just little old me. Ah, so much for fame. And Rod didn't help any. In one city he played the same hall we did, a few weeks before us. And on the dressing room wall he left behind a message: "Ronnie, I told you you needed a proper vocalist for that group."

To this day, people are always confusing me with Keith or Rod. Just a few months ago I went to a concert in New York. Some guy in the next seat turns to me. "Hey, aren't you Ron Stewart?" I said, "No, but I used to play with him." The guy turns to his girlfriend and goes, "This guy here used to play with Ron Stewart." Then he turns to me again. "So what group do you play in now?" "The Rolling Stones." Again, he turns to his girlfriend, whispers, "Now he plays for The Rolling Stones."

But the greatest case of mistaken identity also happened in New York, around the time I joined The Stones. Me and Mick are walking down the street and some girls come running up to us. They completely bypass Mick and say to me, "Hey, aren't you Rod Stewart?" After I signed a few "Rod Stewart" autographs, the kids left pretty happily. Mick and I were laughing our heads off. At least I got mistaken for *some*one. Mick was a bit bewildered by it all.

The first time I toured with The Stones in '75, Keith and I were hanging out in his room at the Plaza Hotel. There's a knock on the door. Keith opens it, just a crack, with his eyeball peeking out. Three people we didn't know. One guy says, "Hey, Keith, we'd like to invite you and your buddies to a party in our room upstairs, directly above yours." Keith closes the door and we thought for a moment. We're alone, got nothing better to do. "Ah, fuck it, let's go on up." We run up the fire exit staircase and knock on the door. "Hi, Keith," they say. Then to me, they go, "And you must be Brian." They were serious. We did an immediate about-face. Those guys weren't our crowd. Probably accountants with the weekend off.

I must admit, though, that I was on the asshole's end of a mistaken identity. I once threw Duane Allman out of The Faces' dressing room. The lousy thing is that I was a real fan of his. But I never saw a picture of him. I just knew that he was one of my biggest influences in playing slide guitar. In fact, later on, his brother Greg told me I had the same hands as Duane. I mean, I loved his music. But I didn't know it was him when he poked his head in the door and said, "You got anything to drink?" I just thought he was some asshole. I went, "Find your own! Fuck off!" And he slid out. I feel real bad about losing my temper with him. The man was decapitated in a car accident a few days or weeks later. I never got to apologize, but I had a wonderful opportunity to pay my respects to him by playing his guitar parts with Mr. Clapton on the "Rainbow Concert" shows. I'm a victim of mistaken identity myself sometimes.

I remember a girl getting really hostile when I casually told her who I was. She didn't wanna believe me. It was a couple years ago in a bar near my house on the Upper West Side of Manhattan. I was sitting there with a friend of mine, Tony, and this really loud girl comes up to me, blabbing away. She's bragging about what a great singer she is. "Oh, yeah," I said to her. "Well, I'm a musician." "That's great!" she yells. "Maybe you can play on my demo tape." I just went along with it. She had no idea who I was. "What kind of experience do you have?" she asks. I say, "I've played on a few albums and did concerts in various parts of the world." She pulls out a pen and starts writing on a napkin. "Good, good," she goes. "Tell you what.

Let me take your name and number and I'll give you mine. So what group are you in? I know a lot of the bands in the city." "I'm Ronnie Wood," I said. "I play with The Rolling Stones." At that point, she takes the pen, throws it in my face, and starts yelling so the whole place could hear her. "What kind of a schmuck do you take me for? You fucking asshole! Find another way to pick up girls!" And she storms out. When Tony and I passed the bar again later that night, the bartender told us that she came back in a little while after we left, and that she asked him if it was all true. He said her face nearly fell off when he told her.

For the most part, though, it's all pretty pleasant. I do go to the supermarket all the time, with no hassles. It's usually good vibes when I'm noticed. Just, "Hey, Woody!" A handshake.

Customs has really improved through the years. When I was coming into New York about the "Dirty Work" time, a customs official pulled me aside: "Damn good album, Woody." Then he says, "You know what cracks me up? You guys used to get torn apart by the old-time officers, but now all we say is, 'Are you gonna tour?' " In London, they don't say anything to me, but at least they don't hassle me. Way back, they used to eat me alive at Heathrow. I tell you, at JFK they're so nice and supportive sometimes they forget to stamp my passport.

One of the drawbacks of fame is that they often make a target out of you. Governments, the press, society. I mean, I nearly got blamed for singlehandedly toppling the Canadian government. That whole time was a mess. We came into Toronto to do the shows at El Mocambo in '77. We were really excited about it. Playing in a teensy weensy club for a few hundred people. The Stones have done it a few times since, but that was the first time. Maggie Trudeau was just a Stones fan. A Stones fan *and* the prime minister's wife. She saw the show, and then came back afterwards to hang out. Nothing bizarre, but it was deemed unbecoming of a first lady. So she quickly made every effort to shed that title. I had no idea of the trouble it would start. I never spent time in Canada before. I figured, "Ah, it's only Canada, how serious could it be?" But her husband was, after all, the prime minister. He could've had me taken out back and shot! The week got off to a shitty start. Everyone was there, except for Keith. We were all rehearsing, since the El Mocambo shows were being taped for our live album. Keith came to

Toronto late, promptly getting into trouble. They arrested his wife, Anita, at the airport. Small traces of what they believed to be heroin and Tic Tacs in her purse. Seriously, Tic Tacs, which they took in for testing. The headlines started. Then the Mounties got a warrant to search Anita's hotel room. But since Keith was in the room when they stormed in, they arrested him instead. Headlines. Keith got bailed out, and we did the El Mocambo shows, with Maggie in attendance. Headlines. "Maggie at Stones Hotel." Blah, blah, blah. Then, Mick, and Charlie go back to New York, and on a plane right behind follows Mrs. Trudeau. Headlines—in Canada and New York. It was all pretty harmless, or so I thought. She was just a nice lady. A fan of the band. She even tried to help Keith out by finding a school for his son Marlon. But the press made a big deal that she wanted *me* out of the whole band, and that there was something going on between us, which there wasn't. It took a while to subside. Maggie returned to divorce Pierre, and he soon left office.

My first true love was a girl called Stephanie. I met her at Ruislip when I was fifteen or sixteen. I never actually, um, fumbled with her. I was so awkward with girls then, sweaty palms and everything. I mean, I simply idolized this girl. She would let me walk her home from school, carry her books and all. That was enough for me. I would run home from her house completely elated, clicking my heels in the air. The great thing was that she used to come to The Nest to see me play with The Birds. And when we started playing some other towns, she would actually drive up with a bunch of her friends, three other girls and this one guy. That is, until they were all wiped out in a car accident on their way to see me.

It was a real blow to me. We were both so young. And the funny thing—well, not funny, really—is that I still remember my father, being the subtle guy that he was, waking me up to tell me about it. As he's shaking my arm to wake me, he goes, "Wake up, Ronnie, c'mon. Something about Stephanie being killed. Come see her uncle downstairs." I must've been in some kind of a daze for those few seconds walking down the steps. But there was her uncle in the living room. "I'm afraid that Stephanie died in a car crash last night," he said. "Ah," I first thought to myself. "So that's why she didn't make it to the gig."

Seriously, though, I learned a lot about life right then. All my friends came 'round and took me to the pub, so I could wash away my tears. There was a cloud over the whole neighborhood. I was so attached to her, I went to see where she'd been killed, the tire marks, everything. It happened on a strip called

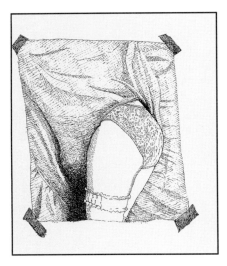

the Henley Fairmile. Weeks after the accident, I had this morbid need to go there. And then after I saw it, I put it out of my mind.

Looking back, I realize that she wasn't the kind of girl I could see myself with today. A beautiful-looking girl, but she needed permission from her parents to do every little thing. I remember standing outside her house when I'd get her home late, and hear her parents screaming at her. I once even hid in the garden to listen to it all. They gave her such a hard time, shouting all this abuse at her. They were one of these higher-class families. But man, they put her through shit.

Linda was another I was mad about. I would just pedal past her house on my bike, hoping to catch a glimpse of her. I was so nervous about approaching her. Finally, a friend of mine got sick of my whining, so he took the initiative and arranged a date between us. I took her to the movies. A double feature. It took me one film to get the courage to put my arm around her. Then, once it was there, I wouldn't dare move it any further. I kept it there through the next film. When we got up to leave, I couldn't move my arm. It had lost all circulation. It was frozen stiff. Naturally, the next day I had to face a barrage of "So, how far did ya get?" from all my friends on the street corner. "Oh, we did everything!" I told them.

With Hazel, I finally mustered up the nerve to ask her out. We went to the zoo. I don't think it was very exciting, but I was simply basking in the glory of actually having asked a girl out. It really boosted my confidence.

Then there was Taffy. She was so gorgeous, I'd come in my pants just standing next to her. She probably wondered why I always had wet legs.

By the time I hit my mid-twenties, my relationships had a bit more depth. (No lewd puns intended.) One girl I really dug then was Patty Boyd Harrison Clapton. (I *think* I got all the names in.) But she and I never got too deeply involved, if ya know what I mean. She was more like one of the boys. Very adaptable, not the nagging type. She turned me on to a lot of great art and literature, like Jerzy Kosinski's works and the photographs of Henri Lartique. I wrote some great songs with her in mind—"Mystifies Me" and "Breathe on Me" from my solo LPs—she was a real heartwrenching type.

It was obvious that she was meant to be with Eric Clapton. I think I made her transition from George Harrison to Eric easier in a way. Eric was a lost soul without her. One night I found him in front of my house in England. He was sprawled in the middle of the road, with just dungarees on, saying how he had to have her. I dragged him inside. After he was calmed down, we hopped in the car and drove to see her. They married in '79.

The whole gang was pretty incestuous, come to think of it. Eric had not long finished dating Krissie when I met her at the Crawdaddy Club when I went to see The Yardbirds (the same night they called me onstage to play harmonica). The romance between she and Eric was fizzling out about then. We got friendly, and just my luck, we got caught out on our first night by my father.

My parents allowed her to stay one night, in a separate room. Naturally, I went for a midnight creep into her bed. We had a quick one, as kids that age usually do, and we wound up accidentally falling asleep. In the morning, my father came in to give her some tea. There was a loud clank when he set it down. I never woke up so fast as then. My eyes popped open and I jumped up. We scrambled to get respectably presentable. My heart dropped. He was pretty cool about it though. All he said was, "Where do you think you are, on your father's yacht?" That was his big line whenever I got out of hand. Krissie and I were so relieved when he started to leave. But then he stopped, turned and said sarcastically, "Well, I suppose I'll have to bring up another cup of tea then."

Krissie and I were together for about eight years before marrying in '73. Her father was a sweet domineering man and started dropping hints like "It's about time." So we did it. Rod was my best man. He said, "I would never get married, but if you're gonna take that plunge, I might as well be best man." It happened in Northampton, where her parents lived. One of the deadest parts in all of England. We shook it up for a day. Rod and my dad got drunk as skunks and sang throughout the whole reception. Songs like "They Can't Diddle Me," "My Wife Won't Let Me," and "Trousers Will Be Worn."

I rarely took Krissie on the road. "No wives" was pretty much a Faces rule, or tradition. So she'd stay home and sunbathe nude in our garden in Los Angeles and do all sorts of things to get rid of the boredom. She'd usually invite one of her girlfriends over. Once, when I was on tour and she was staying at the house in England, the cops raided the place. They were looking for Keith, but he wasn't there. So they crashed their way into the bedroom to find Krissie and her friend sitting there with a tiny trace of coke on the dresser. Of course, it became a big scandal, and when the British tabloids heard that she was found in bed with a girl, they made up this whole story about Krissie being a lesbian. Well, that was pretty fuckin' annoying.

A variety of such annoyances sometimes left me saying, "Ah, women, can't live *with* 'em, and can't live *with* 'em." Things cooled off between us around '76, '77. The three best things she did for me during our marriage were to a) produce one glorious child named Jesse James Wood, b) bring Keith over to the house to work on my first solo album, and c) teach me to swim! I missed Jessie tremendously when I lived in New York until '86, but now we see each other constantly and he blends perfectly with the family setup as it is now.

Anyway, meeting my wife Jo in '77 came at exactly the right time. I was going through a divorce, and so was Jo. We met at a party in England. Come to think of it, Bill Wyman was there. The only reason Jo was there was 'cuz she was about to move into the place where the party was at, Sheffield Terrace in Kensington. She promised her future roommate she'd be there. She was gonna stay five minutes, and split. But I had other plans for her. The moment I saw her from the other side of the room, I said to my friend, "See her over there? She's mine." So then I put on this whole coy bit. I'm standin' by the stereo, puttin' on a Peter Tosh record, when she comes up to me. "Do they have any Osmonds or Bay City Rollers?" she wants to know. It seemed like she wasn't even joking. I couldn't believe it. We had this enormous argument about it. Seriously, folks, The Bay City Rollers? She was coming on like a fan. I have to say, I was intrigued. I'd been fooled! So I asked her things like, "Do you know who I am?" Meanwhile, she was asking herself, "Who the fuck is this cocky guy?" Grabbing a copy of the "Black and Blue" album off the shelf I pleaded, "See, this is me." She remained unimpressed. Turns out she'd seen The Stones once, at Earl's Court in London. A massive arena—she had a great view—yet I was the only Stone she never noticed on stage. Great. She had heard of The Faces, but didn't know I was one of them. Since meeting me, she's picked up a good musical education. At that time, though, all she knew was radio Top 40.

I mean, she thought Lou Rawls was a brand of toilet paper!

So, yeah, she was real evasive at this party. But I didn't give a shit; I was determined. I followed her all over, doing things like hiding behind the fridge. Finally, I hid in the upstairs bathroom. When she came in, I slammed the door and lunged at her. I'm surprised I didn't get slapped. I did get insulted, though. And lied to. She went through this whole story about how she got sick of modeling so she quit for a steady job behind the cookie counter at Woolworth's. The main Woolworth's on Oxford Street. Come Monday, I decided to wait for her there and surprise her after work. I sat there for two fuckin' hours. Thousands of people walked out of those doors, but no Jo. She never worked there. It was a bullshit story to put me off the scent. As far as I was concerned, it only added to the fun. I knew she was

moving into Sheffield Terrace, so I went back there, and that's where she finally came back to.

I guess she was flattered by my persistence. Somehow we started dating. We had a secret rendezvous in Paris. I had to go there for the recording of "Some Girls." I convinced her to fly over and meet me at a hotel: "Be there, and I promise I'll turn up." She got to the hotel to find no Mr. Wood registered. So she took a tiny room upstairs. The place was fully booked, so she got a maid's room or something. She musta been cursing me out, thinking I stood her up. Midnight rolled around, I wasn't there. One, two, three o'clock. She even fell asleep. I didn't show up until 6 A.M. I wasn't helped any by thinking her last name was Howard (that's only her modeling name) while she registered under her maiden name, Karslake. I went through the entire register with a non-English-speaking night porter. He was completely confused. I was beginning to think she stood *me* up. Finally, by the process of elimination, we found the Josephine we were looking for. The porter calls up to her room. Wakes her up. "Monsieur Wood down here." She told me to come right up. When she greeted me at the door, she noticed someone walking behind me. "Oh, Jo, I'd like you to meet Keith." It was then that she was introduced to the inseparable relationship between Keith and I.

For instance, when the limo rolled up to the church for our wedding, seated in the back were me, Jo . . . and Keith. Out stepped the bride; out stepped the groom. And out stepped Keith, munching on some fish and chips, might I add, which he picked up along the way. Y'know, the press has given Keith the image that he's some kind of horrible devil, but he's really one of the sweetest men in the world. Recently, Jo got sick in New York and I mentioned it to Keith over the phone. He was in England. Next day, a box of roses shows up, signed "KR." "It's from my other man," she said. "He's so romantic."

Meeting Jo's parents wasn't too difficult. They approved of me, even though her dad would see The Stones on TV in the sixties and yell, "Filthy! I wouldn't let my daughter marry one of those! They all need baths!" I suppose he became a little more tolerant when he was made head of Lambretta Scooter Society of Great Britain. So he was exposed to a lot of gang fights. The classic Mods and Rockers confrontations where they all battled on those bikes.

As for Jo's mum, she knows how to keep us in check. She was once at our house in Los Angeles about '78, and it was the first time she met Keith. We were sitting by the pool and Keith rolled this huge joint. "Would you care for some, Rachel?" he asked her. "Sure," she went, "I'll have some." She took it and threw it in the pool. We had to hold Keith down to prevent him from diving in after it. So he rolls two more joints and goes, "Here's one for us, and here's one for you to throw in the pool."

The first time I drew Jo was at the PLM Hotel in Paris. Late '77, early '78. Like I said, The Stones were stationed there to record "Some Girls." When Jo and I got fed up with PLM and other hotels, we rented a small apartment. We unaffectionately referred to the place as "Complaining Mansions." It had hardwood floors so that the whole building was like an echo cham-

ber. If you just walked with plain leather shoes on, the people from downstairs, upstairs, the sides, would all ring up and say, "If you must walk around, can you at least take your shoes off?" I stood a fat chance of playing any music there, so I got down to doing some drawings, mostly of Jo.

Obviously, I draw Jo quite a lot because she models for me for free! But moreover, it's because she's got a classical frame. My ideal model. I mean, her body is like a Renoir. Her figure reminds me of the stuff I drew during my formal art training in school.

After having two children and living seven years together, we decided to make it legal. January 2, 1985. It was the natural thing to do. We held off for years so that the kids would be old enough to be page boys and flower girls at the wedding. No, seriously, it was that I simply realized that the grass is no greener on the other side. No matter what girl you're marrying, there's no use thinking there's anyone better out there. 'Cuz if you think there *is* someone better out there, you won't have a good marriage. It won't work. I'm very happy with Jo, as happy as anyone can be with a woman. Perhaps we waited so long because we were a little worried, as most people are, that the romance dies down when you get married. You figure you have your catch, why work so hard? But it hasn't been that way with

Jo and me, just as we hoped. Even Jerry Lee Lewis spotted it. He gave us a whole lecture about how important it is to find that right person (he should know!) and how me and Jo were perfect for one another. I knew there could be no one else but her. Wrap it up, I'll take it!

Marry to make it legal for the kids, we figured, let's do it for the little name sticker on our mailbox. The actual proposal was probably the hardest part. I took her to an outdoor restaurant in Jamaica. A very plush, expensive place called La Ruins, which

was indeed near the ruins of a castle. It was very romantic, under the stars, a great big waterfall off to the side. I tried to be serious; held her hands, looked into her eyes . . . and all she said was, "Where is my champagne?" We cracked up laughing.

The wedding ceremony was tensely comical. The Reverend Peter Crick looked out at the gathering to see the odd rock luminary seated here and there. Rod, Beck, various Stones,

Frampton, Ringo and Barbara. (Clapton was fighting outside the church with Patty. They never made it inside.) Reverend Crick was immediately intimidated and took on an aggressive attitude. "I realize some of you are considered rock idols, but the Bible does not look too favorably upon idols. Perhaps we should refer to the Book of Isaiah: 'Stars, although there are hoards of them, they give off very little light'...Idols take everything and they give very little in response, not wishing to disparage what you're about because far more people have heard about you than know that I exist—or indeed that the Church of England exists." We were very well behaved. But he kept impressing on us that we weren't serious, that we weren't prepared to commit, that this was the only time we were likely to go to church. (Okay, he was probably right about that point!)

Everyone in the congregation was annoyed with his antagonism. At one point, Peter Cook even became a heckler. Meanwhile, my father was sitting there with a look on his face like, "No need for you to be here, Reverend Crick." A friend of mine was so offended he dashed off an angry letter to the Reverend the next day. But he got it back. The envelope read: "Vicar no longer at this address."

Another funny thing was that I forgot to pick up my brothers. They wound up getting there by cab. Me, Charlie, and Keith (my two best men) went to the town registry right before the ceremony. I had to sign the marriage license, whatever. Jo showed up there half an hour late. (Perhaps it was our lateness that set the Reverend off on a bad note.) In the rush I simply forgot to pick up my brothers Ted and Art. So I'm walkin' down the aisle, organ's playing, and there they are, signaling to me: "Thanks for remembering us!"

The wedding was like a tribute to my Mum and Dad's own wedding on Christmas Day, 50 years before. It was a day I'll never forget, one made even more special by my dad making his last and greatest stage appearance—spell-binding everyone in attendance with his own classic renderings of hand picked, special songs and some wonderful jokes for the occasion. Peter Cook gave a marvelous speech. The Dirty Strangers played, Keith and I joined them on guitars, my wife topped it all off by singing "And Then He Kissed Me" center stage, and . . . even the press was great!

8

*A*s I said, I was in the process of divorcing Krissie when I met Jo in '77. Jesse James, my first son, now lives with Krissie in England. He's doing great. He's very well adjusted, has good manners, and is doing well in school.

Jo and I met in 1977. She had a child from a previous marriage, Jamie, who was almost three when I met her. He's two years older than Jesse. Jamie lives with us. It was easy to take him on as my own. He's a special kid. A good art student and doing great in spelling. He's a born leader. I remember, he stayed with me and Jo at a hotel and we'd see him by the pool, bossing kids around. "Get me a milkshake!" But he's not pushy. He's learned a few lessons. Sometimes I allow him to get pretty far, but mostly he knows not to fuck with me. He definitely knows not to fuck with Keith. Keith once dealt him a real reprimand. He was teasing Keith's wife, Patti, all night, making lewd gestures, until Keith felt he went past the limit. He cut Jamie short, picked him up, and practically squeezed him like a lemon. I applauded it. He won't do that again.

Jo and I had our first child together, Leah, in late '78. We were living in Los Angeles then. We then moved to New York, where we first lived downtown, and then uptown. Jo gave birth to Tyrone in New York in '83. Named him Tyrone after the actor Tyrone Power, Tyrone Williams, and a reggae musician named Tyrone Downey. We lived in New York with the three kids for a few years before moving back to England in the summer of '86.

It was a real joy for me to see them all running around with Jesse at our wedding. They get along really well whenever the

four of them, infrequently, get together. It's also reassuring for me and Jo to see them all progressing so nicely. I've been documenting their growth in my drawings.

I'd have no qualms if they wanted to follow in my footsteps. In fact, when Bobby Womack met Jesse, he said he has a good shine for the keyboards. And I've noticed that little Tyrone keeps a good bass drum. Leah too. Jamie sings in the school choir, as I did at his age, but he says he'd rather be a rock 'n' roll manager. The kid's learned young. Perhaps it's the genes he picked up from his natural father, Jo's first husband, Peter Greene, who is a fast talker in the garment and music industries. These days, kids are growing up very rapidly, taking on the best parts of their parents' talents, and becoming frighteningly good prospects. They are all artists. But I don't let them get too cocky. When they do, they get a severe bringing down to earth.

They bring *me* down to earth, too. The kids have been a real stabilizing influence. You have to set a good example for them. You have to give them a lot of attention. I go to their school plays, talk to their teachers, the whole bit of a concerned parent. In fact, I once even wrote a nasty note to Jamie's teacher when he got homework I didn't think was proper for a kid his age. He was only ten or eleven and they gave him this whole thing about Viet Nam. Asking things like "Who was behind the coup . . . ?" And lots of other heavy-duty philosophical questions. I wrote them a stiff note: "This is not the kind of history my son should be learning at his age. Besides, Viet Nam was a big mistake anyway."

Kids have to maintain that sense of innocence. To stay young. There are so many outside, unnecessary pressures on them—like adverts for clothes—that force them to grow up too

early. All of my professional hassles seem like bullshit when I see little Leah putting things in her lunchbox to bring to school —Twinkie, little tiny sandwich, little tiny apple. It just puts things in perspective. Lets you see what really counts.

All of our kids seem to have their heads on straight. Fortunately, they don't seem to give a shit that their daddy is a so-called rock star. Jamie and Leah blend in great with all their other school friends, whom they're always bringing over to the house. Well, maybe Leah thinks she's hot stuff right now since she spoke to Madonna on the phone the other day. She idolizes Madonna. She wears little wedding dresses and jewelry around the house. Anyway, Sean Penn called me about helping him out on a soundtrack, and I casually asked him how his wife was. "Oh, Madonna's fine," he said. At first I said to myself, What, even *he* calls her Madonna? But after all, it is her name. Anyway, I told him how much Leah adores her. When he called again

the next day and Leah coincidentally answered, Sean was nice enough to put Madonna on the horn. Leah was beaming. Her face turned all colors.

To my kids I'm just "Daddy." But as with any father to young kids, they see me as Superman sometimes. They think you can do anything. Tyrone throws his little plastic men into the sewer drain in the back yard and keeps thinking I'm gonna slip through the grates and retrieve them. I wish I *could*. (I'm not *that* thin, but for the kids, I'll try anything.) It must be weird for them to turn on cable TV and see me in a movie like *Let's Spend the Night Together*. I hope that when they see me playing

in front of all those people, they'll get the ambition to do well in whatever they pursue. I think kids and adults have pretty similar concerns, except that kids' are scaled down a bit.

We recently took Tyrone to the opening of a new Disney movie. Afterwards, we went to the party, where he got to meet Mickey Mouse and Pluto. His eyes lit up. It was great. He thought that those men wearing those big costumes were the real thing. And when he came home he just stood on a chair, jumping up and down, plucking his toy guitar and singing, "I know Mickey Mouse! I know Mickey Mouse!" I thought about it. I do pretty much the same thing, stand on a chair and play guitar after meeting one of *my* idols.

I was so awkward as a young-
ster. A real pain in the ass to my brothers, tagging along everywhere like an eager little puppy. That's why they used to kick
the crap out of me so often. They'd pin me to the floor, lean
over my face, and dangle a big gob of spit that they would
somehow suck back up right before it hit me.

My brother Ted is eight years older than me. When he was
in his early teens he loved animals. He collected all kinds of
birds' eggs and had a tank full of tropical fish. One day, for no
reason at all, I just took the eggs and started smashing them,
and flushed the fish down the toilet. I earned many gobs of spit
for that!

My brother Art, who's aptly named, is ten years older than
me. He and Ted were already in college—Ealing Art School—
when I was six or seven years old. Their schoolmates—artists
and musicians—would pile into the house. Wild guys—bohemians with shades, drainpipe trousers, big overcoats, and black
suede shoes with crepe soles. They'd bring over all these nice-
looking chicks and lock themselves in the back room. My parents had a small hatch between rooms, where they could pass
drinks through. I was like a puppy scratching on the door. What
went on in there is nobody's business, but I used to see pictures
of sixteen or so people with their arms and legs draped all over
the couch. I'd say, "That's the lifestyle for me!" I wanted to
emulate my brothers. I got into art and music because of my
sexual attraction to their art-school girlfriends.

If Art was ever alone with a girl and our parents weren't
home, he'd try to get rid of me by sending me to the store. He

figured it'd give him at least fifteen or twenty minutes to get in a heavy necking session. And I, half-knowingly—probably out of jealousy—would say, "Time me. Watch, I'll be back in two minutes." I usually made it back in a minute and a half, much to my brother's delight.

Of course, in my case, even a minute and a half at the store was long enough to get into more trouble. When I was in my early teens I used to go to this one candy store all the time, looking for these candy things called Shrimps. There was this nice little old man behind the counter. He'd naively bend down to get me my Shrimps, the crack of his ass sticking out the back of his pants, while I would reach over and swipe a pack of cigarettes. This went on for months until, one day, I reached over and BASH! The whole framework came crashing down. The old man jumped up. "What happened!" I put this dumb look on my face, "I don't know, it just collapsed by itself." He didn't assume anything. He kept asking, "Are ya all right, young fella?" I said, "Fine."

I never got into any serious trouble. Well, maybe once. I fell in with some rowdy guys and we tore up a train station one Saturday night. We ripped up posters and made a hell of a lot of noise. Hooliganism! We got caught in the act. Fortunately, they didn't lock me up, but the cops came to the house. It was the most embarrassing moment I ever had with my folks. There was a threat of a court appearance, which eventually got called off. I could tell my parents were really hurt. The only thing my father kept saying was, "Your brothers never did this." But I knew deep down they were terrified.

I took a job as a butcher's boy for a couple months when I was fourteen. I'd get there late every day, so I always wound up with the worst bike to deliver the meats on. That was coupled with the fact that the meat always outweighed my frail little body, so the bike was constantly falling over. I'd be tossed across the road, and with me would come the meats. All these people's meats, just rolling in the gutter. I'd pick 'em up and still deliver 'em, picking the pebbles out as I went.

I got another job working for a greengrocer, and another picking potatoes for this Irish slave driver, who made us get there at the crack of dawn. He'd yell, "Jesus Christ and his blessed mother Mary, what the fuck are ya lyin' about for!" He really cracked the whip. Frightened the shit out of me. I wound up singing songs to myself to stay sane. Songs like "Chain Gang."

At that age I didn't take school too seriously. No one did. One time, we made one of our teachers cry. A male teacher. His name was Mr. Levere, and it was during library class. We kept asking him embarrassing sexual questions that he didn't—or couldn't—answer. "Exactly which finger do you use . . ." We bombarded him so hard he finally just broke down and cried in front of the whole class.

I got my just desserts around that same time. I tried so hard to make a good impression on all the neighborhood girls, but I would always manage to mess things up. One especially messy thing happened in church. Having attended schools with names like St. Stephen's, St. Matthew's, and St. Martin's, I obviously had a lot of religious instruction. I said my prayers each night and sang in the choir up till the age of sixteen. Once, all the families were sitting in church, and during the sermon I got sick and started vomiting. I was spouting like a fountain. I nearly drowned everyone in the pew in front of me. ("Pew" being short for "putrid," in this case.) As my mother rushed me out, girls were laughing at me and yelling "Uch!" That incident set me back a few years in the confidence department.

I was really close to my brothers. When I was ten Art went into the armed services for a couple of years. My mother was recently telling me how much I missed him. Ted missed him too. He was like a lost sheep without Art. In fact, when Art would come in on leave, Ted would happily donate his girlfriend to Art and vice versa. I should add that Ted's girlfriend from that time is now Art's wife!

My parents were very loose with me. It wasn't that they encouraged me with my art or music as much as that they didn't *dis*courage me. They were pretty patient with all the loud music and long hair. They already went through it with my two brothers, so by the time I came 'round, I guess they were well prepared. My hair was really long. All they'd say was, "If you wanna walk 'round in public like that, it's up to you, but just realize what it looks like." They gave me and my brothers a lot of rope.

Lots of parents in their position could've been asking themselves where they went wrong. All three sons became musicians and artists, hanging out with wild-looking bohemians, and not

going to work in factories like everyone else. At least Art and Ted settled down pretty quickly. They've been runnin' their own graphic arts company for years. Very successful designing album covers, books, cigarette packages and gum wrappers, race meeting programs—the works! But I, the Woods' youngest son, was led astray for good. I mean, Art and Ted were good enough musicians to go all the way, but they chose a quieter, secure life. They still live within a mile of where they were born and bred. They hardly ever leave there nowadays, socializing with all the guys from way back. As Art told me, "I knew when to hang up my rocking boots." They both still do an occasional gig at local venues, but they wouldn't think of traveling or touring with it. They just don't have the capacity to go abroad like I do. They can't handle the changes in food, it gives them "foreign tummy." The rock 'n' roll lifestyle just isn't for them.

My parents never traveled either. Most of the working-class people from my hometown, West Drayton, just stayed put. Never left. Still live and work there. I think my parents were equally proud of my brothers and me for each of the choices we made. Although I had my doubts at one point. My mother came to "investigate" exactly what her youngest son had gotten himself into, and she didn't seem too thrilled. Actually, it was pretty late in my career. It was '79, while we were recording "Emotional Rescue" in Paris. She made the "big trip" over, her first time ever on an airplane, the only time she's ever left her native England. She drank the pub dry of Guinness—the landlord of the "Winston Churchill" had never had to meet such a demand! I knew I had to capture her on paper. It's not quite "Whistler's Mother," but it is "Woody's Mom." You can see her disillusionment with me in her eyes. She was wondering about her "Little Ronnie." A strange environment for her but she handled it well. She'd look out her Avenue Victor Hugo window and make jokes about all the hookers down there. "Oh, that one in the red dress is back already? She's a quick one!"

I don't think that whole Stones atmosphere would've bothered my father. He was a musician himself. I once "interviewed" him about his experience. As my dad grew older, Keith reminded me to go to England and get his story on tape forever, and be able to play it for myself and my kids in years to come. When Dad died in January of '87, I fully realized the importance of making those tapes.

Keith's found a whole new appreciation for his own father, having moved out of his parents' house when The Stones were starting out. When his parents got divorced, he wound up talking only to his mother and not his father. They didn't see each other for almost twenty years. It was only a few years ago that his father popped back into his life. And now they're inseparable. Making up for lost time. Keith gave his kids a grandfather they never knew they had.

As for me, I always had a good relationship with my father. I'm very happy about that. So the things I got him to tell me on tape were the things that happened to him before I was born, or when I was too young to remember.

Dad's name was Arthur, but his friends always called him Archie, or Timber. From this they called me "Young Splinter."

Archie ran a 24-piece harmonica band. He would say, "It consisted of 24 musicians and one drummer!" They played a lot of pubs in the thirties, but their real love was at the racetracks. They'd play by the winning posts at Kempton Park, Good-

wood, Ascot, all the tracks. Their motto was: "Booze, race-tracks, and women."

He certainly had his share of booze and racetracks. He got his woman one night when my mum walked into the pub where he was playing. He was onstage, in a place called The Crown, when he first laid eyes on her. He put down his harmonica and said to himself, "That's mine." Earlier that night he had won a raffle there for a leg of pork. So his opening line to her was, "This is for you, you've just won the leg of pork!" Romantic, huh? Mum had a chaperone with her. She was allowed to go out on weekends, provided she was accompanied by her mother or aunt. They finally considered Archie acceptable, so they were "allowed" to start courting. They got married on Christmas Day, 1935.

Mum, whose name is Mercy Leah Elizabeth or just Liz, used to work in a place that made machinery parts. She also worked in a floral nursery. And she can really knit and crochet marvelously. Sometimes I forget how artistic she is.

My father was a tugboat captain on the Grand Union Canal, also called the Cut. That's how he avoided having to join the Army. He was one of the people who transported timber and other heavy stuff to waterfront factories. He'd go up and down the canal, from Paddington Basin, London, to Manchester, calling at all the stops along the way. Barging was in our blood. We were a whole family of water gypsies. My parents were the first to actually have a house. The generations before all lived on boats.

What a sense of humor my father had. It helped him get through a lot. I like to think I've inherited some of it from him. Around '80 he had his left leg amputated. The result of thrombosis, a blood clot. When he was first told about it, he asked his doctor, "Why this leg?" The doctor said, "It's a matter of age, Mr. Wood." So Dad inquired, "The other one's just as old!" And after the amputation, he came out telling jokes. "What has two heads, four arms, and three legs?" We were shocked momentarily until he said—

"Mr. and Mrs. Wood!"

He was great at my wedding. He was sitting in the front of the chapel in his wheelchair, leading everybody in singing "The Lord Is My Shepherd" and "Abide with Me." He was ill at the time, but was perked up for this. He had us riveted at the reception, everyone gave him full attention. You could hear a pin drop. He had such a great way about him. A real showman, better than me. He really knew how to deliver a joke or a song. He played his harmonica and we just sat there with our mouths open. It was great.

At a very early age you either take a shine to something or you don't. For me, drawing was all I wanted to do. That, and drumming. I picked up both from watching my brothers.

The drumming bit came as the result of the free-for-alls the three of us had when my parents were out. We'd get out Ted's drum set and make a lot of noise. Somehow, Art and Ted would always wind up fighting, rolling on the floor with fists flying all over the place. They were just fooling around, I suppose, but there *was* a lot of aggression. I'd be shitting in my pants, think-

ing one of them was gonna kill the other. I even developed a stutter during all that disorder. It wore off by itself about the age of f-f-f-five.

But I enjoyed that madness somewhat, and even after they moved out I'd try to recreate some of those free-for-alls by myself. No, I wouldn't try to punch or strangle myself, but I *would* take whatever was left of Ted's set and smash the shit out of it. Then I'd pack it away again under the stairs. Like I said, that's all I wanted to do: drumming and drawing.

One of the earliest things I remember drawing was a bridge. It was sort of like a Van Gogh. (Right!) My specialty was drawing horses. Everyone used to ask me to draw horses for them. I also loved to draw American Indians. I still do. I have a fascination for the wild west. I even named my son Jesse James for that very reason. Perhaps the fascination is because I've always thought I was part Indian. I mean, I do realize I look like one. I've always wanted to trace my roots to see if I had any genuine Indian blood, but I think I'm a little scared of what I'd find out if I dug too hard.

When I got a little older, about twelve, I met up with some minor success as an artist, on "Adrian Hill's Sketch Club," a TV show. Every Friday I'd run home from school so that I could glue myself in front of the telly to watch Adrian Hill. Schoolkids would send in their drawings to him, and if they were good enough, he'd show 'em. My drawings got on a couple of times. On Monday, I was the biggest thing at school. One year I won a contest from his show, and they put some of my stuff on exhibition at St. Alban's. I even got a spot in the newspapers; all really encouraging to me as a young artist.

I went to St. Martin's Secondary Modern in my neighborhood. That's the equivalent of high school in the States. It was at St. Martin's that they really developed my art talent. But because I excelled in that one area, I missed out on a lot of other things, like wood shop, metal shop, or chemistry and biology. I had history, but failed it. I aced the final exam, but ... I got caught cheating. I had various dates written all the way up my arm, and I got busted. Simple as that. It was the only time I cheated and the only class I flunked. I got my O-level in art, geography and literature. That's like a degree or diploma. O-level is good, but A-level is best. I achieved my A-level in art a year before the normal entry age. So I was off to Ruislip Manor, a sort of junior college that specialized in art. It was totally my choice. I mean, seeing as how I came out of secondary modern—as opposed to "grammar school," which was largely for the upper class—I wasn't expected to get any further education. Working-class kids like me were supposed to leave school at sixteen and go straight to work in a factory. I don't know if my parents thought it was a curse or a blessing that all three of their kids went to college rather than punching the clock.

Doing well at Ruislip got me into a "real" art college: Ealing, just like my brothers. Students had a lot of freedom at Ealing. You could smoke in class and there were hardly any teachers around. They'd just leave you alone in the class lots of times. I

guess they figured that if you came this far as a serious art student, you'd either do your work or you wouldn't. *Your* life. And to tell you the truth, almost everyone I knew at art school became a musician instead. They gave up any hope of becoming a professional artist.

Like I said, it was a pretty big deal for a working-class kid to go to college, but what did you get out of it? Once you left art school there was no chance to earn any money. You gave up learning a trade, and art jobs were not easy to come by. The only one I got was as a signwriter. Four pounds a week, which was equal to about $8 then. Eight bucks a week! It was sort of an apprentice job, but it was the only logical step after graduating from Ealing. After a couple months, I knew I had to get out of it. Creatively, signwriting isn't a great form of expression. You're told what to do. It wasn't worth the schlepp. I did some signs for real estate brokers and the local refrigerator store. Also, a window poster for the local pet shop. My swan song was painting ads on the roof of the local football (soccer) stadium. It had a corrugated roof inclined over the stands, so that you could see it from the other side of the field. It looked great, especially from an airplane. It was my Michelangelo bit. I was scared shitless to go up there every day, but it only took four weeks instead of four years.

My first breakaway from that unreachable dream of being a graphic designer came when I went on a couple of serious interviews and realized I wasn't wanted. It was out of my league. To this day, however, both of my brothers make their living as graphic designers. Back then, getting into the business involved a lot of politics. You had to know someone, be part of a clique—or part of a union, especially in scenic design. My brothers knew a lot of people, so they got plenty of commercial art jobs. It was the same thing with Charlie Watts. He started as a tea boy in a design studio, and was allowed to work his way up. He eventually got his own little desk there and became established, like my brothers. He had a tough time giving that up for The Stones.

I, however, became obsessed with music. I was already brought up on jazz, but the success of rock 'n' roll made one think again. I figured, There's some money to be made here, a gold mine. Look at Elvis. But I never went into music counting only on a gold mine. I was attracted to it when I saw that those

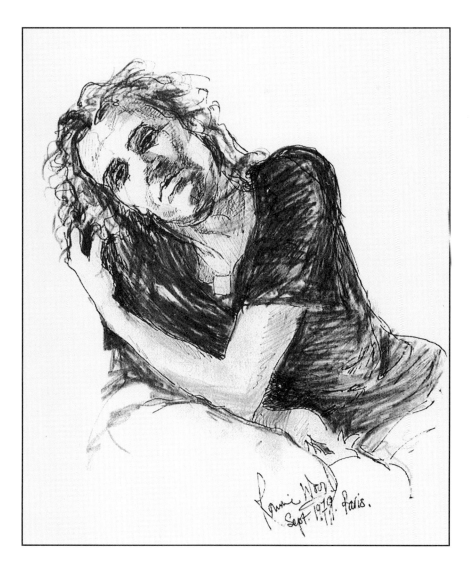

guys did what they did with style.

I used to see Keith Moon around Ealing. He wasn't a student, but he lived near the train station. He was *always* a maniac. Even before I was friendly with him, I could see the fun he was having with The Who and the creativity extending from Townshend impressed me. I also watched a girl named Linda Keith around school a lot; at the cafeteria, wherever. She was a student, real gorgeous, but she was going out with Keith, as in Richards. I used to say, Well, if she's going out with a Rolling Stone, then hmmm. Girls look at them differently. I simply realized that I'd do a lot better for myself, financially and socially, by drawing crowds to my gigs instead of drawing pictures on a canvas.

As you can see, I've drawn a lot of funny little imaginary characters and scenarios. Most of them are depictions of unpublished poems Rod and I wrote during the Faces days. But today, the bulk of my work is portraits, where I try to capture my subject as accurately as possible without overworking the image. Make it look like the person. Of course, someone like Jo, whom I've probably drawn more than anyone, will occasionally say, "Uch! That doesn't look like me at all!" But I'll answer her, "Well, that's the way you looked to *me.*" That's the way I saw her at that moment. Accurate, but subjective. In the way a photographer can capture the mood of an entire sequence of events in just one frame.

Rembrandt was one of my earliest influences. I remember copying a famous self-portrait of his. It was in '60 when I seriously began studying art in secondary school that my attention had been captured by Rembrandt, Leonardo, and Michelangelo. Soon to follow were Mantegna, Dürer, Daumier, Lautrec, Cézanne, Picasso, Braque, Turner, Delacroix, Titian, through to Arthur Rachaur, Beardsley, Roland Torpor, Escher, Magritte, Lynd Ward, Ralph Steadman, Frank Frazetta, Dudley D. Watkins, W. J. Linton, my brothers, Henry Wolf, and Charlie Watts. All of these helped shape my delivery of the line into what it is today.

I was greatly influenced by the impressionists' use of color, the Japanese use of the brush-stroke, and the German and Italian techniques with wood block.

I was fortunate in learning some techniques by watching my brothers. They taught me a lot, and really took the time to guide me through things. They were my greatest living artistic influences. Art loved doing caricatures, and Ted instructed me on shading, perspective, and proportion.

William Blake wrote in the early nineteenth century: "Painting is drawing on canvas and engraving is drawing on copper and nothing else, and he who pretends to be either painter or engraver without drawing is an impostor."

I keep in touch with the work of particular contemporary artists. I liked a lot of Warhol's stuff. I'd take little hints from him. We used to bump into one another at parties in New York. He was over at my house for my birthday in '86 and I naturally dragged him around for a walking tour of my work. He was very encouraging. I had a good chance to talk with Ralph Bakshi when he was working on the "Harlem Shuffle" video with us. We got around to discussing some of the great pioneers of animation, such as Tex Avery. I've hung out with Peter Max quite a bit, whose work I was unfamiliar with until recently. I love his "Statue of Liberty" stuff. Peter and I got into some good exercises at his studio, painting together. We'd just stand alongside one another, no preconceived ideas, pick up the can-

vas, pick up our brushes, and yell, "Let's go!" I learned to let go.

You never can say when the inspiration to draw is going to hit you. It can happen halfway through a raisin toast. Or you can be on a train and get so possessed that you cut off a piece of someone's shoe leather to draw on. Perfect strangers. I've done that. The desire hits, and wham! That's why a lot of my drawings are on little scraps of paper. Some of Rembrandt's greatest works, I bet, were done on the back of unpaid bills.

Then again, there are other times when I'd *like* to be drawing, but I'm lacking either inspiration or motivation. That can be pretty frustrating if it goes on for months, as it can. So you try to maintain an energy that you can release on command when the time is right.

Tension provides a good impetus for painting. You let out your emotions on paper rather than confront someone in person. It's like all the drummers who smash their sets rather than beat their wives. Every song you play and every picture you draw releases a little tension. A few times Keith and I felt like killing people, but we picked up our guitars and wrote songs instead. That's how we came up with "Fight," "I've Had It with You," and "One Hit to the Body." Oh, yeah, we've all been spared long jail sentences by being able to play our music.

So music and art are equally satisfying in that way. If I have both of them in front of me, I'm not sure how I make the choice. Sometimes I do both at the same time. When I would come down the stairs to my basement in New York, if I walked straight, there was all my artwork. If I cut a right turn, I'd be in my studio with all my guitars, drums, 12-track machine. A lot of times I ran back and forth from one to the other. I do the same thing even when I'm on the road. I always intermingle my art and music, letting one be conducive of the other. I keep my travel art supplies in a trumpet case. I also ram my paint brushes down the end of my tenor sax. It's all very economical.

I did make art a definite priority when I went to San Francisco a while back. I went there for three separate weeks in '84 to study under a professor at a workshop. I churned out a lot of stuff, like my portraits of Hendrix, Marvin Gaye, and Muddy Waters. I worked feverishly every day from 10 A.M. to 5 P.M. All the productivity is what led to my first exhibition in Dallas, in December '84. But my main reason for going out to San Francisco was to learn about monotypes and woodcuts. I did thirty monotypes and three woodcuts in those three weeks. Since there was nothing goin' on with The Stones then, I was able to commit myself to trying new artistic media. New to me, anyway.

They're pretty old media, actually. Monotype may sound like a disease that should be stamped out, but it is actually a printing process where you apply an oil-base paint onto steel or some other hard, smooth surface, and then press that image onto pourous paper. When you peel the paper off, ninety-nine percent of the image is transferred from the steel plate to the paper. Simple enough. It's almost the same theory as those lick-on tattoos you had when you were a kid. But you only get one print from each painting of the plate, and thus the name monotype. As I said, ninety-nine percent of the image has left the plate and gone onto the paper. But there is still that faint image —actually called a "ghost image"—of what you originally painted, stuck on the steel. So if you want to make another print, you can carefully repaint, or shall I say, trace over, the one percent image remaining on the steel. And the great thing is that if you didn't like certain parts of your original, you can slightly alter it by painting over the "ghost" until it comes out perfect on the next print. So you can see how a gradual process of improvement is possible in a series of such monotypes. (For instance, look at the Lennons I did. At first, I painted it onto the steel. Made a print of it, and saw his face was too fat. So I went back to the steel plate and repainted it, but this time I thinned out his cheeks. Then I made another print, went back to the plate, and improved it *again*.) You can keep adding minor adjustments after making each print. But as I said, it's called a monotype because you can only get one print at a time from that steel plate. As you can also figure out, the monotype print is a mirror image of what you originally painted on the steel plate. In other words, when I originally painted Elvis on the metal plate, he was playing guitar right handed. But after the paper was pressed onto the plate and then removed, it came away with a reverse image, so that Elvis became a lefty.

Woodcutting is a harder way to make prints, but once you've set it up, you can make plenty of prints at one time from the same original. And unlike monotypes, where the image virtually disappears from the plate with each print, woodcuts endure. In

fact, there are prints being made from woodcuts that were done in the 5th century. Woodcutting, by the way, was the first illustrating technique used in printed books. (I'm sure Bill Wyman remembers that.)

In order to do a woodcut, the artist first draws an outline of his design on the smooth surface of a block of wood. Then, with small knives and gouges, he cuts away the wood between the lines he drew. It's painstaking work, but if you do it properly, cutting out the unwanted space of wood on each side of a line, the lines that result are almost like pen lines that are raised off the wood. You gouged out the parts you didn't need. It's a simple theory, really, just like the image on a typewriter key— I mean the part that hits the paper—or one of those rubber stamps you use to stamp your envelopes or bills with. The raised image, when inked, is the part that reproduces when pressed onto paper. The areas of wood you cut away, obviously, don't show up. It's different from monotype, which is done with the use of a steel plate or some other flat surface. Here, with raised wood, there are certain textures you get on the print that can't really be done with other media. (Look at Chuck Berry's hair, for instance.) But since it is such hard work, I've only done three of 'em so far.

Learning new media, like monotyping and woodcutting, gave new life and dimension to my work. I feel the same way about Caran d'Ache pencils, these great water-soluble pencils from Switzerland. They've made me more prolific because they're so easy to manipulate. You can draw a line in a flash, much better than regular pencils. They give you a lot of freedom to execute the way you want. They're especially helpful when there's a call for detail in your subject.

Of course, I do stick with the traditional charcoal. The old 6B pencil. Charcoal is one of the oldest drawing media. It can help you give the impression of rapid movement. Masters like Rodin and Matisse used it so well for that purpose. You can also smudge it pretty easily if you want, just by licking your fingers.

I've done some work with pastels as well. They have a certain purity of color that I like, which I don't think you can find in oil painting. Plus, they have a good immediate response on the paper.

I'm pretty unorthodox with a lot of my stuff. Pretty untraditional. I mean, I seldom use an easel. It's nice to have something to rest the canvas on, but if it's not there, I'll improvise. Likewise, I'll grab anything to paint with, no matter what it is. For this Jagger painting, I needed yellow, which I didn't have, so I used mustard. (Probably because I used up my yellow paint the last time I had hot dogs.) And for the gold in the painting—if I can call it a painting—I used the tinsel stuff from a crystal champagne bottle. I'm not gonna let anything stand in my way.

10

*Y*ou gotta have a sense of humor. Life is too rough without one. Thank goodness I was brought up in a family that kidded around a lot, that dry sort of British wit, remarks coming from the side of your mouth.

But I love some of the old slapstick masters. I can watch Chaplin or the Marx Brothers for hours. (I sometimes do.) I felt compelled to draw some of my favorite comics, from both schools, old and new. Just looking at their faces on my wall makes me happy.

I'm really glad I got to know some of them, like Peter Cook and Dudley Moore, and the guys from Monty Python. I love to collect comedy albums and videos almost as much as collecting music.

The ability to make people laugh is a gift. What a great form of communication comedy is. It's a pity that some of the best comedians are miserable inside. Belushi was a perfect example. It's like they're out there sacrificing themselves, making every-body happy except themselves. Then again, at least they're get-ting money for it. 'But there are lots of assholes you meet in the world who *don't* get paid for being jerks, 'cuz they don't know they're being jerks. That's what separates the miserable *profes-sional* comedians from the miserable *unintentional* comedians.

GROUCHO MARX

Ahmet Ertegun took me and Eliot Gould to Groucho's house a few years before Groucho died. It was a big Jewish holiday—Passover, I think—so he had his whole family there. Nephews, nieces, grandchildren. Little kids running all over the place. Groucho was sitting at the head of a U-shaped table arrangement, and he would occasionally grab one of the kids running by, put them on his lap, and pretend he didn't know them. "Now what did you say your name was?" He was also wearing a party hat. (Yes, I'm certain it wasn't a yarmulke.) What a delightful guy.

Anyway, the funny thing is that when he first opened the door to greet us, his immediate words to me were, "That's the silliest haircut I've ever seen." Ahmet said to him, "This is Ron Wood."

"Who?"

"Ron Wood."

"Oh, of course, I've seen all his films."

"No, he's in the band The Rolling Stones. He's a big fan of yours. He has all your movies."

"That's nothing. I have all of his albums. Now what group did you say he was in?"

Throughout the night, all he kept saying was, "That's the silliest haircut I've ever seen." Meanwhile, Eliot and I were speechless. Everything Groucho said was so sharp, he'd hack you to pieces. It was

hard to keep up with him. So I finally said to Eliot, "I'm goin' up to say goodbye." I was reminded of a scene from *At the Circus* where everyone is about to get up from a table until Groucho keeps saying, "I think I'll have one more cup of coffee," and everyone sits down again, up and down, up and down. So I jokingly say to Groucho, "I think I'll have one more cup of coffee." But he refused to play along. Instead, he just mumbled some gibberish at me, and I felt like a complete idiot.

But he did confide in me one thing before I left. He said, "Look at all this. I'd give up every dollar I ever earned if I could just get one erection."

CHARLIE CHAPLIN

The little tramp! A wonderful presence, a classic person. A purist and a walking example of comedy's main rule—that comedy is always at someone's expense. (Usually his!) Such a sad little man, really. That's why I used the juxtaposition of his two faces.

Of course, I'm too young to have seen any of his movies when they came out in the theaters. The closest I got was by way of my auntie Ethel. She used to play the live music behind the silent movies in the theaters. (You know, I can probably think of some rock 'n' roll movies that should've been done that way.)

MARILYN MONROE

I share the same birthday as her, June 1. Reason enough for me to draw her, but I regard her as a special subject in that her image has been so over-exploited. I drew Marilyn because Jo and I were gonna put her on T-shirts, assuming that many people would like to wear her on their bodies.

Tony Curtis spoke of her when he and I used to talk and draw together in London and Los Angeles. He said he first met her when she was hanging out in the parking lot of Para-mount Studios when he was in Hollywood with Cary Grant. She'd stick around—in the days of the big studios—and hope she'd be discovered in the parking lot. Well, I don't know what she did (maybe park some cars!), but it obviously paid off. And although she got a little spoiled mate-rially, she always wanted peo-ple to give her something more —to recognize her talents. Mind you, this is coming from Tony Curtis. He had a much better view of her than I did.

JOHN BELUSHI

I knew he was a contender for the "fatal brigade." Basic-ally, he was a very nice man. But a very pathetic creature, like true comedians usually are. Very lost in their personal lives. He did have a lot of re-spect for people, including me, always seeking advice about personal problems, how to handle his fame and the acco-lades. I mean, the praise that *Time* magazine and the music trades heaped upon him was all very sudden. I remember how he always wanted to bring his and the Blues Brothers' success to my, Keith's, and Mick's attention. We'd say, "You should let *us* congratu-late *you,* John, not ask us to tell you how great you are." But that was his charm. He had a tough time deciding whether he should be himself or a fa-mous headline. Perhaps I should have called this paint-ing "Tears of a Clown."

He made a good model for this one. He was in the middle of doing the film *1941,* and had just messed up a stunt. He fell off the wing of an airplane. A doctor prescribed Demerol, so he was in a pretty eased state of mind. Very mellow. He just sat there giving me a nice op-portunity to capture him. Hence the title, "Belushi on Plane Killers."

He used to come 'round to see Jo and me a lot when we lived in Los Angeles. He'd make a point of visiting when-ever he was in town, wasting no time in proposing marriage to Jo every chance he'd get. He would wait till I fell asleep or was out of the room, and then get on his knees and propose to her. He was always after Jo's behind. Good clean fun. Jo and I used to keep him out of trouble. Of course, that's not according to a certain Bob Woodward, but that's where his *Wired* book was completely wrong. We may have had some fun with drugs, but John never took any cues from *me.* He knew exactly where he was going, what he was doing. I used to keep him sane, pulling him off whatever he may have been on at the time, saying there was no future in it.

I saw it coming in a way, like Keith Moon. You'd never have predicted his demise, but it was no surprise. A tragedy. No one could alter the course that his destiny was going to take.

DAN AYKROYD

He and Belushi were a great team. It wasn't only great to see them together for the comedic value, but also because Dan was a solid figure in keeping Belushi together. You always knew John was pretty safe when he was with Dan. It was only when Belushi went off the leash that he'd find himself in danger.

The two of them used to own this bar in New York that we'd all hang out at, especially after they'd get off the show on Saturday nights. There'd always be bikers hanging around. Dan still hangs out with a lot of 'em. He's one himself. It was kind of touching to see Dan riding his bike, leading the funeral procession.

The last time I saw Danny he was cooking. It was after the MTV Awards in '84. During a party held at the Hard Rock Cafe, which Dan's part owner of, I open the door to the kitchen and there he is with a chef's hat on, flipping burgers. Cheeboigahs!

WHOOPI GOLDBERG

She's so talented. I first met her in Miami when I was working on Don Johnson's album. We were marooned together. Don took us out to sea on the "Miami Vice" boat. Me, Jo, Mr. and Mrs. Stevie Ray Vaughan, and Whoopi. Don stopped the engines for a few minutes (while passing a hospital) and then tried to restart them. No way. All these sparks start shooting out. "So this is the boat you were bragging about, huh, Don?" We all start ribbing him. Immediately, everyone's a mechanic. Jo and these other girls are all hunched over the engine with their asses sticking in the air, thinking they know what they're doing. We wound up drifting into the nearest dock, which belonged to a home for senior citizens. We all jumped off the boat, and went inside to make phone calls. We sat around the reception area for an hour, waiting for cars to pick us up. All these people were walking past us in brightly colored clothes, shorts, black socks, carrying bridge tables, folding chairs. Not one of them recognized us. They didn't know who Don was and they probably thought me and Stevie Ray were hoodlums. Finally, this whole crowd gathers around Whoopi. "Hey, aren't you Whoopi Goldberg?" I think it was a blow to Don's ego. But surely he has to maintain that low profile to carry out all that undercover work with Tubbs, making Miami a safer place to live and play bridge.

RICHARD PRYOR

To get the right feel for this portrait I used crushed-up bronze in the paint. It gave it a lovely shimmer—much like him! Nah, I shouldn't joke about what he went through. I'm real glad he's only part of the *nearly* "dead people" section of this book. He's a survi-

vor, like The Stones, though his survival has been a bit more public. Like yessir, a lot of people run down the street on fire without getting in the papers! I know I have!

I've never met the man or been to one of his concerts, but I think he's got a great way about him. He's a good artist with his words. He strikes me as a big loon.

I've heard a lot of stories about him being the original Mr. Paranoid. He'd be in the back of a limo on the floor

yelling, "Turn right! Turn left!," thinking he was being followed by every car behind him.

Mick told me about the time he and Richard were down in Trinidad partying for days during the Carnivale. They went back to Mick's house, and as Mick was preparing eggs, Pryor's snooping around the place. He opens the door to the bedroom and sees Bianca lying there naked. "Hey Mick," he goes, "you sure got some great maids around here!"

My worst example of being targeted was when me and Jo got tossed in jail for six days in St. Martin. We went down there for a peaceful vacation in February 1980. We brought the kids and their nanny, a great lady named Jaye. As soon as we got off the plane, I could tell they had their eyes on us. I had this big ghetto blaster that made me stick out in the crowd. One sleazy customs officer wound up following us all the way to the house we rented. He eventually asked Jaye out on a date, took her to some chicken take-out place, but when he parked the car at some lovers' lane, Jaye demanded to be taken home. After that, he had it in for us.

Anyway, a couple days later we're at the casino, and we meet two guys. One of them was a croupier. They followed us and tried to sell us some coke for such and such thousands of dollars. I said, "I'm on holiday with the kids and that's the last thing I want." Then one of the guys asks, "Can I borrow your car? Mine's got a flat." I said it was okay.

But these guys borrowed our rented car to pick up some coke. Then, when they returned it, unbeknown to us, they tied up a bag of coke behind a tree in our street. We didn't see it, but our neighbors did. They reported the license plate number of the car, and the next day the cops showed up.

When the doorbell rang and Jaye told me the police were downstairs, I figured it was just another complaint about the music. I was upstairs playing my Dobro guitar in my cut-off jeans. As I ran downstairs I dropped my Dobro and it broke in half. I walked up to the cops with a sad face and said, "Look, my Dobro is busted!" They didn't care. They said they were there to search the place. No warrant, of course: I said to them, "Go ahead. You can search all you want, I've got nothing to hide." But one of those guys from the night before had left his jacket on the couch. It had a little coke in it. Upstairs, the same thing: the other guy left *his* jacket with some stuff in the pockets. I said, "Look, you won't believe this but . . ." I tried to convince them. "If this stuff were mine, do ya think I'd be dumb enough to leave it around when I heard you ring the doorbell?" They didn't answer that question. In fact, they didn't say anything at all, except that me and Jo had to come down to the station. I figured they'd come to their senses when we got there. I was so naive I said, "Sure, we'll be glad to help you out." I didn't realize that Jo and I were the prime suspects.

Next thing I know they're asking me to empty my pockets and remove the laces from my sneakers. All I had were my shorts, socks, and shirt. The guy tells me to walk down this pitch-black corridor. Shoves me in, slams the door. "I'm in the fuckin' slammer!" Meanwhile, Jo was going through the same thing. All we could hear was our kids crying, down the hall.

Six days in the fuckin' shit hole. When I looked through the bars of my cell into the courtyard, I could see a lizard, a mouse, and a roach all looking at me. It was like a human zoo. Our cells had no beds. Just a concrete block. No pillows. A bucket in the corner that they'd collect once a day if you were lucky. Worse was the fact that that lousy customs official would walk by my cell with a big grin on his face. They were all in cahoots.

The actual jailor guy wasn't so bad. He'd occasionally ask us if we needed anything. Cigarettes, magazines, books. One book he brought me mentioned The Stones. I yelled to him, "Look, this is me!"

It was lights out at ten, up at six. For breakfast, coffee and a roll with moldy salami. "Don't eat the meat," I kept yelling to Jo across the courtyard. I never got to see her, but she was having a pretty miserable time on the other side. When she would leave her cell to take a shower, she had to pass some other inmates, big guys playing dice. Thank goodness she wasn't raped.

We met one really nice guy in there who, by coincidence, I had once met before on a Stones tour. He helped us pass notes back and forth, sticking them on the end of a broom handle. He arranged it so that if I climbed up at a certain time, I would be able to see Jo's hand waving at me. That's the only way I knew she was still alive. All his notes would say, "Destroy this note." It was like "Mission Impossible." One time, the jailor allowed him to have an ice cream cone. I was dying for a lick, but he was too far away. He stuck it on the end of a broom handle, stood on top of a garbage can, and tried to get it over to me. My mouth was salivating, the cone was teetering at the end of the handle, it was inches away, and . . . plop! All over the floor. The guy got hell for it, too.

After a lot of wheeling and dealing we got out. Since we were on the Dutch side of the island, one of their laws was that I had to use a Dutch lawyer. All my lawyers flew in but they were told, "You can talk till you're blue in the face, but it'll do no good." Finally, my lawyer befriended a local lawyer. We got a chance to go before a judge and give our stories to him separately. The stories matched up and they let us go. Also, they had pulled in those other two jerks by then. It turned out they were big international movers. Just before I got out, I saw the croupier. He looked like shit, as opposed to his usual suave, smooth-talking self. They asked me, "Did this man try to sell you drugs?" Without hesitation, I looked the guy right in the eye and said, "Fuckin' right!"

We were sprung. No fine, no explanation. We still don't know how or why it all happened or exactly who was behind it. As we were leaving I turned around and said, "Can I pay for my stay with my Midnight Express card?"

ERROL FLYNN

What a fuckin' prankster! I once knew one of his daughters, Rory. Also, I went to see one of his houses off Mulholland Drive. I was looking to buy a new house. I forgot the name of the guy who owned the place at the time, but he wrote that song for Rosemary Clooney, "This Old House." Which is pretty ironic, because he took me 'round "that old house" which was incredible in that it was planned out and wired up. Errol had catwalks built in, two-way mirrors, speaker systems in the ladies' room. Not for security. Just that he was an A-1 voyeur. He picked up on everything in that house.

He had some pretty risqué parties, as everyone knows. I heard that at one party he dug up this dead body. Wait, I'm wrong—the guy was dead, but before he was picked up and sent off, Errol got hold of the corpse and propped him up next to the pool. It was one of those fat actors, like Sidney Greenstreet. I forget. Anyway, he says to all these young chicks, "Hey, do me a favor. Go show my friend over there a good time." And they go sit on his lap. Next thing . . . "Aah!" There's this big shriek, and the girls are running across the hills of upper scenic Mulholland.

It's an odd story, especially since rumor has it that Flynn "died with his boots on." Or shall we say, he died while, er, "in the act." At least he went out smiling. But it makes me wonder what the poor girl (or girls) went through. Probably thought it was one of his fuckin' pranks!

BILLIE HOLIDAY

If you don't know when Billie Holiday's singing, there's something wrong with your ears. What a brilliant character. Before her, no one heard a blues singer sing it soft, polished. All the others, like Mama Thornton, were shouters. I mean, Martha Reeves used to stand ten feet from the mike. Billie immediately demands a great deal of respect from anyone with an ear, or eye, for music.

My brother Ted introduced me to her music. He's something of an authority on her, which is perhaps why he didn't like Diana Ross playing her in the movies. He felt Diana was too naive to be a blistering hopeless case like the original. And I must agree. At the same time, it'd be a shame to paint Billie as a drug addict and let it overshadow her singing. Because nothing could surpass her rare talent. She was one in ten billion.

PETE TOWNSHEND

Ah, Trousers, what a bloke! I always had a great respect for him 'cuz he had a great respect for *me.* I mean, he didn't have to, at the time. It was way back. The Who had already made it on the club circuit, getting all the great weekend gigs, while I was just starting out. But he'd tell people how much he thought of me, which was more than I thought of myself back then. It really boosted my self-confidence.

Yet, for the most part, he was a real belligerent type. Very destructive, smashing things up all the time. That was more than just a show biz gimmick. He was always fighting with Ronnie Lane, or Moonie, or Daltrey. Him and Keith (Richards) had a brief exchange of words—mostly violent words—a few years back. After lending The Stones his A-1 roadie, Alan Rogan, for our European tour, Townshend called up Keith one day and said he wanted his roadie back. Right in the middle of the tour. "You bastard!" Keith yelled. "You said we could have him for the full tour!" Keith hung up on him.

Everything was fine, though, when he came up onstage at our gig at the 100 Club in London. When he came onstage he suggested we do the old song "Harlem Shuffle," which was just being released as our new single then. But it wasn't some

nice gesture on Pete's part. You see, *he* had just recorded the song himself. And although we have no proof, we think he got wind that we were covering the song on "Dirty Work," so he decided to rush it out before *we* had the chance to release it. It's the kind of sardonic, classic Townshend move that's still his charm.

DON JOHNSON

When we met at Live Aid and he asked me if I'd play on his debut album, I jokingly said, "Yes." I didn't think he was serious. But Don has credibility in the world of rock 'n' roll. I mean, he's not like David Soul, some actor who just woke up one morning and said, "I'm gonna make a record." Don used to write songs and jam around with the Allman Brothers. It was a treat to go down to Miami and do the sessions with him.

A month later he sort of hid out in my house in New York when he was going through all that negotiating bullshit over his contract. I think he wanted $150,000 an episode. Anyway, he phoned up the show's producers from my house and told them, "If you don't give me what I want, I'm gonna join The New Barbarians and we're gonna start off with a half a pound." Half a pound of what, I don't know, but it was quite a threat. It scared the shit out of 'em and he got his money.

A few weeks later he mailed me a gift from Miami. I don't even know how it could get through the mail. A pine box with an engraving, "From one Barbarian to another." I open it up and it's a Smith and Wesson .45. A strange gift, I think. As you can imagine, Jo was simply delighted, what with a house full of kids. It didn't come with bullets, though.

All Don drinks lately is Moussy, that alcohol-free beer. He actually convinced me to try one. One case, that is. Seriously, Don's really cleaned up his act. He told me that he stopped messing with drugs and booze 'cuz he got sick of having to call his friends the next morning: "Gee, I'm real sorry about breaking that 15th century vase of yours. And, oh yeah, I'm also sorry about fucking your wife."

To get a good likeness of myself I planted my face down on the glass of a Xerox machine and made a copy. The hardest part was keeping my eyes open. But my main concern was the radiation. Then again, I suppose it's only a small price to pay for a perfect image of myself.

Actually, I must admit, I normally use a mirror when drawing myself. As you can see, I've done self-portraits during various stages of my life. In fact, I know I drew myself in the womb, but I just can't seem to find it. Maybe I left it there.

It's not difficult for me to do self-portraits. It's like drawing any other subject except that, this time, it happens to be me. My face is just another thing for me to draw. I'm able to remain pretty objective and strive for a certain kind of accuracy. If your face is riddled with bad points, you can't hide it. I've had enough wear and tear to feel lucky that I'm still alive. Sometimes I think hard about that.

It's all just a matter of taking cues from your body. You'll know when it's time to stop with booze or dope or staying up six nights in a row. But it's up to you to adhere to the demands of those messages.

Most people do drugs out of boredom. Musicians off the road will try to fill in something that looks like a boring day. Lots of people are also deluded into thinking it makes them more creative. Arthur Conan Doyle, Sigmund Freud, and so many others throughout history are said to have done some of their best work while under the influence. The point is, someone like a Keith Moon would take a whole bottle of pills. I would not. It's just common sense, something Moonie obviously ignored!

When I was in my teens, going to all these clubs in London, my friends and I would gather at the railway station. "I had twenty ups," one guy would say. "How about you?" And I would answer, "Oh, yeah, I also had twenty," even though I had only taken one or two at the most. Even if those guys were lying and took just half as much as they said, it's no wonder they were so out of their fuckin' brains.

Anyone with intelligence knows you can always jump down from a futile challenge somehow. "Here's five pills. You better take all five." If there was no way out of it, I would just down one pill and keep the other four under my tongue. Then I'd spit them into a hanky when they weren't looking. I did that lots of times. I never had the tolerance to take five Quaaludes all at once.

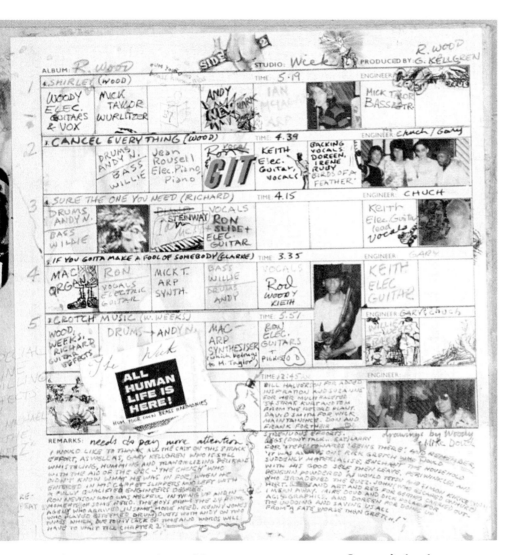

I've known a lot of lunatics in my time. I won't bother to mention their names, even though most of 'em are no longer here to read this. The annoying thing about those people was that they thought *I* was crazy for not taking part in it all. That's fine, I'm willing to play the "bad guy." No matter how many people tried to persuade me, and no matter how out of it I was, I have never injected anything into my arm. To me, it's alien. Even when Keith (Richards) was going through his awful times, he was at least never stupid enough to shoot into a vein. Even when people thought Keith was far gone, I always knew he had too much sense to be careless. He knew his tolerance and he knew exactly what he was taking. Accidents happen when people don't check out what they're taking, when they don't know what it is. When China White came around, it looked like coke, but was actually smack. Keith was an intelligent drug user, if there is such a thing. And thank goodness he's now off that shit altogether. He really cleaned up his act. I saw many people trying to keep up with Keith. Only the grace of God kept them alive. Too many people wind up dying because the people around them don't know how to handle the situation. I've learned that if people overdose, you must keep them awake. If you let them fall asleep, it becomes an eternal sleep. I've walked lots of people around the room to keep them alive.

There are some other obvious rules. If you're gonna shoot up, don't be stupid enough to pop some pills at the same time. Don't mix needles and pills or alcohol with pills. With booze, you don't mix the grape and the grain either, like brandy and bourbon. I've become a preacher on many occasions to save lives. I saved Belushi's life several times. I've saved my own life on a number of occasions. The biggest step was checking myself into a clinic a few years back. (Contrary to sensational reports, the decision was completely mine and Jo's.) I have too much responsibility to myself, my wife, my kids, the band. It took me four decades to build this life. I'm not gonna tear it down for a silly night of overindulgence.

*Y*ou get scars in whatever business you're in. There are executives who get ulcers, and there are accountants who escape the pressures by getting blitzed on the weekend. In our case, it's worse, though. People come in and out of our lives like hit-and-run—they might be there for one night of heavy partying, but then they can take as long as they need to recover. But we have a whole new bunch of people coming in the next night. I've suffered a lot of wear and tear on my body by staying up night after night. Then there's another show to do and you go through it all again. It tells on your body after so many years, and that's a scar I carry around.

There's also the airplanes, the cars, the dodgy situations. It takes a chunk out of you each time, and any one of those trips could be your last. With stuff like that, you have no say. Going down in a plane crash is an act of the pilot, an act of God. I say, when your number's up, your number's up. Don't matter if you're on a plane, train, rocketship, or bicycle. Lots of people won't fly, thinking it cuts down the odds. As for me, I've always put my life in the hands of fate. Everything I do is controlled by it and, for the most part, I've fared pretty well. It's like giving up smoking and being hit by a Lucky Strike Truck. I am still here, after all, and I've done just about everything I've wanted to do, played in every band I ever really wanted. I've had every lucky break, such as joining The Stones after wanting to for so long. There's only one thing I still haven't accomplished in my career: I'd like to sit in the audience at one of my shows. Not watch it on video, but be right there in the seats. Now that's difficult.

When they interviewed him on cable TV, my name was mentioned. He said, "Ronnie—I helped raise him." He calls me and Keith "the two finest youngsters I know."

JERRY LEE LEWIS

The Killer! Yeah! I first met him a long time ago at the Palomino Club in Los Angeles. He was fabulous! Blew the roof off the place. I never saw such an electrifying performer. After his show, Mick Fleetwood, and Dave Mason and I went back to meet him. It was great. We got nice treatment from his manager. We became great friends. I played with him at the Rock N Roll Hall of Fame ceremony, on the same stage as all these other idols of mine. I kept saying to myself, "I can't believe I'm up here." (Earlier that night, I couldn't even muster up the courage to say hello to James Brown, who was sitting at the next table.) I mean, it wasn't my thing. Keith was up there. He was one of the award presenters, but I didn't even do *that.* Yet people kept pushin' me up. Finally, Bill Graham got me onstage. It was great.

Afterwards, Neil Young and I took Jerry Lee over to Keith's house with us. We played the tapes of the "Dirty Work" album, which wasn't out yet, and he sat there and said,

I kept wondering to myself, "Why am I here with these guys, taking part in a video about the birth of rock 'n' roll?" "I wasn't there," I told Carl and Jerry Lee. And he snapped back, "You're here now, boy!" And I said to myself, "I *am* here!"

Jerry Lee's license plate says, "No wife." He's been through half a dozen, I think, so bachelorhood is a rare situation for him but one he seems to crave. He's a strange guy with women. While we were shooting the video, a female assistant comes into the trailer and says, "Mmm, you smell great, Jerry Lee. What's that you got on?" He said, "I got a hard-on, but I didn't know you could smell it!"

"That's rock 'n' roll." This coming from the guy who did "Great Balls of Fire" was all I needed. I thought to myself, "I don't give a damn if 'Dirty Work' sells ten copies. I already got *my* royalties."

It gets better. Months later, in June of '86, he rang me up to tell me to come down to Memphis to be in a video with him for Carl Perkins' song, from the Class of '55 album,

"Birth of Rock 'N Roll." It's about the early Sun Studio guys. The song was already there, they just wanted me for the video. We shot all the scenes outside Sun. At one point Jerry Lee looks up and says in a very bewildered way, "I just realized where the fuck we are. Elvis and myself once rode down that street on a motorcycle stark naked, with a cop chasin' us on a horse.

ELVIS PRESLEY

I never met him, but I once made a fool out of myself trying to. He was in a Memphis hospital shortly before his death and it was quite obvious the man was going off the rails. So I wanted to say hello before it'd be too late, and talk to him about music. I went there on my own, but the nurses wouldn't let me past the first floor! I waited for a while, then realizing it was hopeless, I gave up my last chance to meet him.

I did see one concert of his in Vegas. I stood next to Sammy Davis Jr. in a long line waiting to get in. At that show I really got into Elvis' sense of humor, his tongue in cheek delivery. My true appreciation for Elvis grew in the years preceding his death. That's why I wanted to get into that hospital, desperately hoping to make up for lost time. My admiration for Elvis gradually built up through the seventies, a magnifying process. And it really began as the result of listening to his guitarist Scotty Moore. Scotty was such a hip, masterful player in a very subtle sort of way. During the sixties I didn't pay attention to Elvis when he was making his "GI Hawaii Clamshake" movies, and when I was a kid in the fifties, I was still seeped in the jazz idiom because of my brother Ted. So Elvis did not have an initial impact on me when he first came out.

The other thing is that... well, never mind. Oh, all right. I was intimidated by Elvis. Not Elvis per se, but the people who liked him. My cousin Dougie, for instance, who was a bit of a criminal type, loved Elvis. I associated Elvis with the violent get-togethers of youth gangs. Dougie would be blaring "Hound Dog" from his radio while having his face bashed in—or while doing the bashing. It frightened me away from liking Elvis. Whenever you listened to Elvis 'round where I lived, you stood a good chance of going through a plate-glass window.

CARL PERKINS

Carl got Jerry Lee Lewis to ask me to be in the video for "The Birth of Rock 'N Roll." They were shootin' it in Memphis. I was on that plane like a shot. I got to Memphis, drove up from the airport, and there's Carl to greet me. What a nice host. If anybody knows about the birth of rock 'n' roll, it's him. He told me that in the early days, Chuck Berry used to ask him for advice on his songwriting. "Hey, you think these lyrics work?: 'Gonna write a little letter, gonna mail it to my local d.j.' " That let's you in on the other side—wow, these guys were human. "Blue Suede Shoes" and Chuck's songs are like monuments— sometimes you forget there were real people behind them.

The Beatles loved Carl. They once threw a party at some castle, and invited him. He knew who The Beatles were, but wasn't quite sure what they looked like. He went to the party and just stood around awkwardly. Then he noticed some guy staring at him, keeping his distance. Finally, the guy—who was totally in awe— walks up to him, and says, "Hi, I'm Ringo. I'm one of your hosts tonight." Then Ringo clanks his glass, and goes, "Ladies and gentlemen, the guest of honor is here." They pretty much threw the party just to meet him.

KEITH MOON

He was lucky to live as long as he did. He tempted fate every day of his life. He was a lot of fun to be with (although sometimes you could have a heart attack just watching him). He was a real big pal of mine. Before his death, he and I were planning a TV series, a variety show. We drew up all these massive plans, and antic- ipated guest stars like Marlon Brando and every luminary you could think of. (It was going to be produced by Gene Rodenberry, who created "Star Trek.")

I really miss him. He was a real gent. Very polite to my mum. He gave me a Piaget watch before he died. I had never received such an expen- sive gift. Mind you, he was drunk as a skunk when he gave it to me. So I said to him, "Look, if you still wanna give it to me tomorrow, okay. But not now." Next morning, he woke up bright and early and the watch was mine, complete with purchase and customs documents.

I never knew where he got his money from. I must have seen him spend over four times his prospective lifetime

In '75 The Stones used a big stage for their tour. Enormous thing that opened up into a lotus flower. The Stones sold it the next year. Moonie bought it for his front lawn.

income. And that's *way* before he died. It was just part of the reckless attitude that finally did him in.

He lived on the deep end. It's a wonder he didn't manage to impale himself, what with all the daredevil leaps I witnessed. Jumping out of windows, busting through walls. One night on tour with The Who, he got a little lonely at the hotel, so he decided to visit Entwhistle. But he took a shortcut. He hacked a hole through to Entwhistle's room and climbed into bed with him. The following morning, the hotel staff noted that the room he was originally in was completely devoid of furniture. He had tossed it all onto the front lawn. An empty room—no wonder he got lonely in there!

Hotels loved Keith. Once, he literally camped out in the lobby of the Beverly Wilshire. They had no rooms left, so he sent his chauffeur to fetch his tent from the trunk. He pro-ceeded to pitch his tent right in the lobby. I already had a room there and was walking by, just at that moment. I helped try to hammer the tent pegs into the carpet.

I frequently used to see him make his way around hotels by going on the outside. Climbing and leaping from terrace to terrace until he reached his destination.

Another time, he showed up at a hotel by driving a car right up the front steps, through a plate glass window, and straight on through the lobby to the reception desk. Then he got out and nonchalantly asked the receptionist, "May I have the keys to my suite, please?"

SID VICIOUS

I like the way he did "My Way." I think he had something to say, if not something to punch, while he was alive. I also liked the fact that he was such a creep.

The other Stones and I never resented how The Sex Pistols and other punks put us down. It was obvious to everyone how influenced they were by bands like us. It was just an attitude they devised. "Never mind the bollocks, let's get it in for the old farts." But Billy Idol brought Steve Jones to my house recently and he was a real fan. Yet if this were '77 and he were in public, he'd be the first one to slag us off. Mick had a flat 'round the corner from Johnnie Rotten and they got along quite well. That defiant bullshit was all image. Public image, ha, ha. But I guess Sid took it a little too far. Yes, Sidney, you did it "your way."

BOY GEORGE

An interesting face. I met him a couple years ago on New Year's Eve in St. John's Wood. All these British bands like Madness were there, with all their families, parents, and aunties. George—or shall I say, Boy—or better yet, Mr. O'Dowd—was real nice to my kids. Gave them dolls and toys. He and Keith have this running thing. He met Keith in Jamaica and said, "What's this I read in the papers about you calling me a bag lady?" And Keith answered, "Well, you do look like one."

BOB MARLEY

Obviously the man did something right to become synonymous with the word *reggae*. Rastaman Number One. It was a treat for me to play onstage with him at the Oakland Coliseum in '78, I think. Yeah, that's right, 'cuz Jo was pregnant with Leah. Anyway, I had just met Bob at his gig the previous night. So I figured, *I'm playing with that guy tomorrow —even if he doesn't know it.* Moments before the show, I cleared it with his band, and then I stumbled up to Bob. "So far, you're the only one who doesn't know I'm coming onstage tonight." He said, "If you can do it, great. If not, don't fuck up." Once onstage, he gave me a look that said I passed with flying colors. Red, green, and gold.

I lived in Los Angeles in the late seventies. I sold my house, The Wick, in Surrey, England, and figured I'd head to the States. Since I was born and bred in West Drayton, a London suburb, Los Angeles seemed like the closest atmosphere to it in the United States. I was wrong. But I had some wild times out there. Neil Young lived down the road. That guy knows how to greet a neighbor. He didn't bake a cake or ask to borrow sugar. He just shows up at my doorstep one day, rings the bell, and there he is, guitar in hand. All he says is, "Let's go for a ride in my Greyhound bus." He was serious. He had the bus parked behind his house, complete with bedroom, bathroom, kitchen, and music room. So I grabbed my guitar and we took off. We wound up playing for days. He was the person who came up with the name The New Barbarians for my pickup band. If he didn't have other commitments, he'd have been part of the band himself.

Anyway, I became very close with his roadie, this guy named Sandie. Fantastic friend. He used to drive around in a converted ambulance that he bought. Well, one day, October '76, I had company at the house. Company as in Mick Jagger, Linda Ronstadt, Governor Jerry Brown, and Warren Beatty. I was still married to Krissie, who was extremely pregnant. She starts to go into labor right then and there and everyone starts to panic. (I could see the headline: "Governor Delivers Rolling Stones Baby.") By sheer coincidence, the doorbell rings, and it's Sandie. "Hi, everybody. Does anyone need anything, I got the ambulance parked out front." "Yeah!" I shouted. "How about a ride to the hospital!" So we were off to Cedars Sinai. We laid

Krissie down in the back, and me and Mick got inside. Warren Beatty hung onto the back of the ambulance 'cuz he said he wasn't comin' to the hospital with us. Instead, he jumps off a few blocks away to visit some girlfriend. "You're welcome for the lift, Warren. We're only having our first child here!" Anyway, Mick was great in the hospital. Real supportive. He and I slept on these uncomfortable chairs in the waiting room, and he also went in a few times to hold Krissie's hand. Then he helped me fill out some papers to allow a Caesarean section.

A couple years later, Jo gave birth to Leah at the same hospital. This time, it was Keith's turn to help out. He came with us to the hospital and started driving the nurses crazy. I was a little more relaxed this time, so he coaxed me into putting on surgical outfits—robes, masks, gloves—and walking around like doctors. When the nurses asked, "Which one of you is the father?" we kept saying, straight-faced, "We are."

We nearly lost our house in Mandeville Canyon. I remember having been up for about five days. So when I finally got to bed, it felt great. Half an hour later a guy rang the doorbell, screaming like a madman. "Wake up! The canyon is on fire!" So I grabbed some of my paintings, a few guitars, threw 'em in my jeep, and hit the road, Jack. I just sat there looking up at all the black smoke in the sky. It was frightening. But two blocks from my house it took a detour, completely missing us. It stopped four feet in front of Ian McLagan's house. Neil Young's place was destroyed, while mine was left untouched.

That's not the only near-tragedy the house survived. Must have been '78 or '79 when me and Keith are lounging around my pool. (Oh, by the way, the house used to belong to Esther Williams. You'd think she'd have a great pool, but it was pretty lousy. A disgusting kidney-shaped pool.) Anyway, we both smell something pretty awful. "Keith," I said, "you're a smelly bastard!" And Keith says, "Woody, have you forgotten your potty training again?" Then, I look up. There's this brown sludge coming down the mountain! The cesspool had broken, and it was dripping down like lava. (Lavatory in this case.) It seemed like the whole town's waste was about to be heaved on my front lawn! So I run inside, throw on my boots, and grab shovels and umbrellas, hoping that I could push it back up somewhere. Keith, of course, says, "I'm not goin' anywhere near that shit," and scurries inside. It was like a horror movie!

TINA TURNER

Hot legs! She's a pal. Every time I see her, she gives me a big cuddle. In the old days, she used to think I was Keith and she'd give me this great big kiss. I, of course, would wait 'til all her niceties were finished before I'd say, "It's not Keith." And she'd go, "Well, I enjoyed it anyway."

Somehow I got it to change course, this time headed straight for Esther Williams' kidney. Within a few minutes Keith was pleased to see that I had a pool full of fertilizer. A fun summer of swimming was had by one and all!

ger legs go running by. I said to myself, "Hang on. It looks like he's leaving." I yelled to him, but it was too late. His ass was just a blur. We were stuck there, enjoying ourselves, yes, but realizing we had a gig in Seattle that night. After numerous attempts by Rod, Mac, and everyone to get ourselves out of there, I crawled up to Ike, practically on my fuckin' knees, and pleaded with him. "Please let us out of here, Ike, 'cuz we got a gig tonight." Finally, he signaled his henchmen to let us out.

I think it was a plan of Mick's to have us miss our gig. Or maybe he thought we'd be trapped there forever and it'd cut down the competition, that sly dog. Ike's a lovely guy, but we were married to him for a day and a half, so I hate to think what it was like for Tina all those years.

BOB DYLAN

That man stole my blankets! It all happened this strange night in Los Angeles, one of the first few times I ever met Bob. I was in the midst of doing some work at Shangri La Studios with Eric Clapton. He was making his "No Reason to Cry" album there. One night, when I didn't show up, Dylan came by to help Eric. I'm on the phone with Shangri La and the girl says, "Oh, Bob Dylan is here and he's playing bass on one of your songs." I said, "What!" So I dash down there and wind up

IKE TURNER

After spending over a day with Ike Turner, I realized why Tina stayed with him as long as she did. He probably wouldn't let her out! Must have been around '72 when Mick brought The Faces over to jam at Ike's studio in Torrance, California, where he had all those locks on each room. Sophisticated

shit, you know, dial a certain phone number and the door would lock or unlock. Ike had all these guards standing 'round, *big* muthafuckas, and we were his "prisoners" for well over a day. Mick somehow slid out through the side door after a few hours. He had his fun. (Most of it derived by watching *us* squirm.) I was in the toilet and I see these Jag-

spending the next day and a half with Bob and Eric.

Shangri La's like a bordello, maze corridors, beds and everything. So when I finally go up to get some sleep, I walk in my room, and my blankets are gone. I see the curtains blowing—the window's open. I look out into the distance, this big field. Dylan was like miles away, with some chick in a tent. A girl with a cast on. But not only had he made off with this wounded bird, he made off with MY blankets! That's when I realized he was a strange character.

But, wow, we spoke for hours in the bathroom at Shangri La. He asked me if I preferred playing with Clapton or with The Stones. I told him it's great to be in a band. He said he'd always wished he was part of a band. "All the weight falls on me. I wish I had a bunch of friends to split some of the pressure with."

That's why it was great to do Live Aid with him. And he was so humble and appreciative about it. In fact, *I* was the one who initiated it. Three days before Live Aid, Bob didn't know we were gonna do the gig with him, but *I* did! So I had to lie to Keith and get him to my house under false pretenses for the first rehearsal. "Hey, Bob wants us to play with him in Philly." "Anything to help Bob," Keith said. So me and Keith are hashin' out some Dylan songs in my kitchen, when in walks the man himself through my front door. First thing he

says is, "Hey, are you guys gonna go to the show on Saturday or stay home and watch it on TV?" Keith then began to strangle me. "You bastard!" he went. "What did you get me 'round here for! You wasted my time! We got an album ('Dirty Work') to make!" Bob then went to the toilet, so I got hold of him when he finished, and he said he'd love it if we did play. I said, "Great! Just go down and tell Keith right now that *you* want us to do it." He runs downstairs, grabs Keith, bam, "Would you play this gig with me?" And Keith goes, "What the fuck do you think we're here for? Of course I would!"

We ran through the whole Dylan catalog at my house. Keith would play all these riffs and Dylan would ask, "How'd you know all that?" Keith would answer, "I stole it from you, you schmuck!" We wound up teaching *him* what he taught *us* in the first place!

Apart from the fact we couldn't hear anything on stage, we had great rehearsals. If only we could've heard ourselves as much as we did when we were rehearsing. But as we were facing out at the show and literally blowing in the wind, the sound was going out and just getting lost. A shame, because Bob sang so well, and the lyrics to the songs were so poignant and relevant to the event.

Looking back, I know that I didn't understand some of his stuff when I was younger. I al-

ways considered him a great poet and songsmith. But I only grew to appreciate him as I got older. I'm still just scratching the surface of all his influences, like Woody Guthrie and Hank Williams.

I first met Bob at a Faces party in Los Angeles, a place called The Greenhouse. It was just after I did my first solo album in '74, which didn't exactly set the world alight. But I really hoped certain musicians, like a Bob Dylan, would take notice and appreciate it. Anyway, no one knew Bob was at the party. He was underdressed and just blended in. Everyone thought he was a photographer. Then he just emerged from the crowd, came up to me, and said, "I love your album." Pow! I was blown away! We had a five-minute conversation and I remember Peter Grant coming up to us and saying, "Hi, I manage Led Zeppelin." Bob shot back, "Hey, I don't come to you with *my* problems."

Lots of people have this weird thing meeting Bob. I remember backstage at The Last Waltz concert Muddy Waters telling Pinetop Perkins, "We gotta meet this guy Bob Dylan. I think he's pretty famous." And when Neil Diamond got off stage, he said to Bob, "You'll have to be pretty good to follow *me*." Bob snapped back, "What do I have to do, go on stage and fall asleep?"

I heard that at the Bangladesh concert, Jessie Ed Davis was just sitting innocently

the summer of '86. Three nights, about an hour each night. (Got to meet Bob's mother backstage. Wonderful lady.) And of course, we've got tons of tracks on tape that may one time see the light of day—things recorded in studios, basements, hotel rooms.

We've been good friends over the years. He started hanging out at my house in Los Angeles during the late seventies. (Jim Keltner, the great percussive drummer, would bring him over.) Thank goodness Bob never preached to me about religion. I told him, "I'm real glad you dropped the Prophet of Profit thing, Bob."

JOHN LENNON

Such a wonderful man. I guess everyone already knows that. He was a great comedian. I learned a lot about him from other people I've spoken to. Ringo and George loved him so much. Paul, too, probably, though he has a tough time admitting it.

I only got to meet him once, around '78 or so—him and his wife, Yoko. The Stones were staying at the Plaza. I got an unexpected knock on my door, and there he was. "Hello, Ron, I'm John, this is Yoko." And he bore gifts! He brought a White Horse whiskey bottle for Keith and cardboard Yorkshire terriers that were used as adverts for Black & White scotch for me. Booze and cardboard dogs! I loved it.

backstage, munching on an apple, when he saw Dylan across the room. He thought Bob was giving him all these nasty looks. Jessie was really bothered, getting real intimidated, trying to guess what would happen next. The tension was mounting. Finally, Dylan approaches him: "Can I have a bite of your apple?"

I love Bob. I'd do anything for him. Lent him my guitar when he did the Letterman show. Once, I almost flew all the way to Stockholm just to play on stage with him. I had a tight schedule at the time. I was just gonna touch down in Stockholm, play a couple hours, and take off. But it fell through. I had rehearsals for an upcoming Stones tour.

I've since done a lot of guest work with him on his albums and onstage. I had a great time playing with him and Tom Petty at Madison Square Garden in

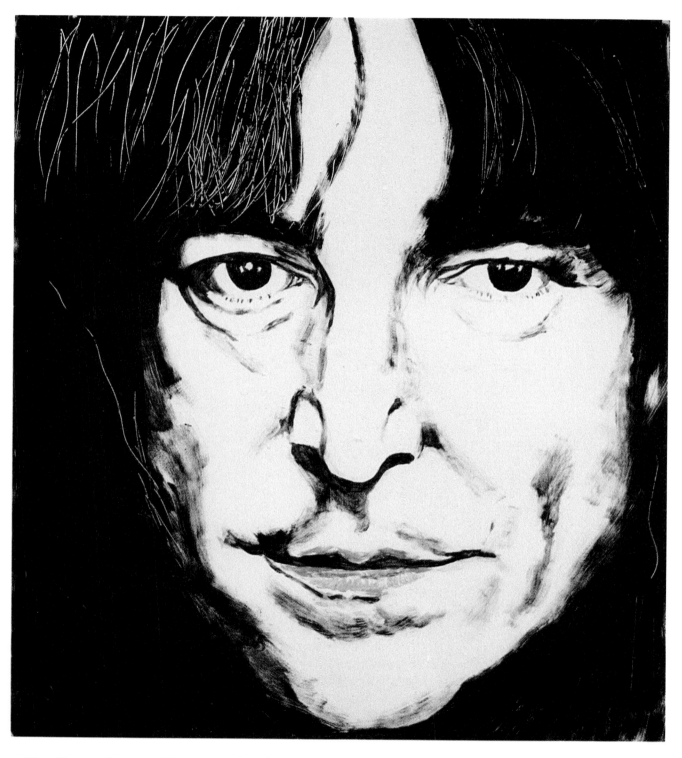

We all went down to Charlie's room. It was the only time Charlie's ever gotten a hotel room complaint in his life. He had just bought a wind-up Gramophone, with one of those big horns, and he starts playin' all these 78s. The phone rings... "If you don't turn that noise down..." Next thing we know, security is bangin' on the door! It wasn't even late

RAY CHARLES

A frail-looking man, but very powerful. You can hear *that!* He likes to keep to himself. I think he's a little pissed off at life. I can't blame him. If I were blind, I'd be bitter too. Jerry Lee Lewis says I've got him pegged wrong, but I still think Ray and Jerry Lee share one obsession—women.

Jerry Lee and I did a show with Ray in New Orleans for cable TV recently. I could tell Ray was a little uncomfortable playing with some musicians he never played with before. So, to put his mind at rest, I approached him and said, "Ray, I won't play too much on "Drown in My Own Tears." I don't know it well enough." He appreciated that. Then he asked me to hold his sweaty towel. I did.

I had a lot of fun that night. Came right home and drew this picture. I once scribbled another one of him, but I can't seem to find it. I was on an airplane and he was sitting a few rows ahead of me. He's sitting by himself, with the headphones on, rocking back and forth. He even got up and danced in the aisle for a few minutes. In a world of his own. When he sat back down, I ripped out a clean page of a magazine and sketched him. Just the back of his head, ears stickin' out, with headphones.

and the music wasn't even that loud. I suppose we were just talkin' real loud.

Later, John got the sudden urge to get high. So he took whatever, started to sweat, and then, wham! For the rest of the night he was down for the count. And Yoko was just sitting there knitting. It was lousy 'cuz it prevented me from talking any further with him. But at the same time, it was good to see his system was real clean if his tolerance was that low.

He's another one who left us too early. It's one thing when someone offs themselves by being stupid. But when someone like Otis or Buddy Holly go in a plane crash, or something they didn't ask for, that hurts. For John, the plane crash came on 72nd Street.